Creating Miracles

A Practical Guide to
Divine Intervention

REVISED EDITION

Carolyn Godschild Miller, PhD
Foreword by Terry Lynn Taylor

An H J Kramer Book

published in a joint venture with

New World Library
Novato, California

An H J Kramer Book
published in a joint venture with
New World Library

Editorial office:	Administrative office:
H J Kramer	New World Library
P.O. Box 1082	14 Pamaron Way
Tiburon, California 94920	Novato, California 94949

Text design and typography by Tona Pearce Myers

Library of Congress Cataloging-in-Publication Data
Miller, Carolyn Godschild.
Creating miracles : a practical guide to divine intervention / Carolyn Godschild Miller.—Rev. ed.
    p.   cm.
"An H J Kramer book published in a joint venture with New World Library"
Includes bibliographical references.
ISBN-13: 978-1-932073-16-4 (pbk. : alk. paper)
1. Course in miracles. 2. Miracles. I. Title.
BP605.C68M55 2006
299'.93—dc22   2005028325

Revised edition first printing, March 2006

ISBN-13: 978-1-932073-16-4
ISBN-10: 1-932073-16-7
Printed in Canada on acid-free, partially recycled paper
Distributed by Publishers Group West

10   9   8   7   6   5   4   3   2   1

Contents

Foreword

Creating Miracles is like a spectacular diamond, reflecting light on a truly interesting subject from its many facets. It is one of those books you can't put down because it contains amazing accounts of real-life miraculous occurrences presented as if you were there. I love that. It is enjoyable, heartwarming, skin tingling, and emotionally satisfying. And it becomes a valuable handbook that you will need to keep nearby after you read it.

Because Carolyn Miller is a conscious social scientist and experimental psychologist, we get a view of miracles from a very grounded perspective. It is not easy to take something as subjective as divine intervention and open it up for examination without ruining the wonder of the actual experience. But Carolyn has added dimension to the wonder, which left indelible images and feelings in my psyche. When a book stays with me in retrospect and becomes something I reference in my own thoughts, as this one has, then I have a book that I will keep forever and return to again and again.

Creating Miracles reflects a true "life's work." What this means to us as readers is that we get to share in this work and reap the rewards. The rewards of a study such as this don't depend on whether you end up "believing" in miracles — for some, believing may not come easily where things like miracles and angels are concerned. However, you will gain something of great value: a profound awareness of the love all around you, all the time — a love that facilitates change, acceptance, and knowing. Know this: you are not alone; angels, guardians, and miracles exist everywhere, and you are truly loved.

Carolyn has expanded an important part of the big picture for us. *Creating Miracles* offers us cogent evidence of the miraculous and tools for personal exploration so that we, too, may expect a miracle!

Terry Lynn Taylor,
author of *Messengers of Love, Light & Grace*

Acknowledgments

This book is very much a group effort, drawing as it does upon the miraculous experiences of numerous friends, students, colleagues, and readers. The extraordinary courage, creativity, and compassion these people displayed in the face of grave, and even mortal, danger has been a great inspiration to me. In order to safeguard the privacy of my story-tellers, I have generally changed their names and altered identifying details. For the same reason, I will not acknowledge each one by name here. Nevertheless, I want to express my profound gratitude to everyone who provided a precious piece of the puzzle. The picture becomes clearer with each new contribution.

I also want to thank Georgia Hughes and Kristen Cashman of New World Library and my copy editor, Jeff Campbell, and to express my deepest appreciation to Hal and Linda Kramer of H J Kramer Inc., who published the 1995 edition of *Creating Miracles* and copublished this one with New World Library. Linda, in particular, provided much-needed encouragement and direction. Without her, this book would not exist in its present form.

And most of all, I want to thank my husband, Arnie Weiss, who contributed to this work at every stage of the process, and without whom *I* would not exist in my present form.

Introduction

*D*o miracles really happen? How will you ever know for sure, unless they happen to you?

When I wrote the 1995 edition of this book, I thought there was a strong possibility that research on the healing effects of prayer, or the cures deemed "miraculous" at Lourdes and elsewhere, might eventually yield convincing scientific evidence for divine intervention. Since then, I've come to understand that the scientific method is, by its very nature, incapable of shedding much light on the supernatural. The credibility of alleged miracles will always be a matter of personal judgment. We accept the possibility that divine intervention has occurred when we feel it is *sufficiently unlikely* that the result could have been achieved by any other means. But in the end, each of us must decide for ourselves what constitutes "sufficiently unlikely." There are no events we can know for sure will *never* be explicable in naturalistic terms.

Accordingly, there will forever be at least two perfectly good nonmiraculous explanations for any supposed supernatural occurrence: 1) *It actually has a perfectly ordinary cause we just haven't yet identified*, and 2) *It didn't really happen —* at least, *not the way it was reported*. Perhaps the witnesses got their facts wrong, as witnesses so often do. Or maybe they are simply lying. The fact that so many alleged miracles *do* turn out to be bogus upon closer examination lends credence to this hypothesis. To skeptics, the possibilities of fraud or an honest mistake will always seem more plausible than any amount of evidence that something "impossible" actually occurred.

The approach to miracles we'll be taking here, however, does not rely upon the impossibility of the end result, but rather upon the extraordinary state of mind shared by people who experience narrow escapes from highly dangerous situations. We'll see that an oddly peaceful and compassionate altered state of consciousness reliably seems to precede life-saving reversals of fortune.

Further, these true stories of ordinary people in extraordinary circumstances fall somewhere between "the impossible" and "the everyday." While the positive outcomes were certainly *surprising* given the way events were shaping up, they were by no means *incredible*. I think you'll have little trouble believing that such things could really happen.

Why is the mental state of people who experience narrow

escapes significant? Because spiritual traditions from around the world agree that entering a peaceful, loving, and forgiving meditative state is the very thing that makes divine intervention possible. This shift from fear or anger into unconditional love is widely believed to be a necessary condition for miracles. Thus, the people who shared these stories seem to have spontaneously followed the procedure mystics say will permit miracles, only to have a turn of events that is arguably miraculous occur.

The interpretation that these surprise happy endings were actual miracles is usually mine, rather than the storyteller's. A person may have many complex psychological motives for asserting that he or she has been the object of divine intervention, but most of the people who told me of their narrow escapes made no such claims. Although some saw the hand of God in what happened to them, most regarded their experiences as nothing more than fantastic luck.

And what makes me think they were anything more than that? Because when we look at many such incidents together, a pattern emerges. What at first seemed to be only random lucky breaks suddenly come together to form a new category — one made up of situations where an endangered individual enters a peaceful, fearless, and unconditionally loving meditative state, follows inner promptings, and then finds a bad situation taking a surprising turn for the better. As we examine these events, we'll consider alternative explanations for what happened, as well as some advanced thinking within modern physics that may help to explain how a shift in consciousness really could alter the course of events within the physical world.

Best of all, after we've explored this procedure for creating miracles, you'll be in a position to try it out and decide for yourself whether or not it works. If it does, your own experience will provide compelling evidence for the existence of divine intervention — evidence that you personally can trust whether or not anyone else agrees with you.

Science is never going to prove or disprove the existence of miracles — not because there are no good reasons to believe in them, but simply because those good reasons are based on personal experiences rather than publicly observable events. Besides, unless you are able to see miracles at work in your own life, how are they ever going to be real *for you*?

Chapter One

Are Miracles Really Possible?

Fail not in your function of loving
in a loveless place made out of darkness and deceit,
for thus are darkness and deceit undone.

— *A Course in Miracles*

ational headlines recorded a miracle of deliverance even as I was writing this book in the spring of 2005. Nothing but more death should have followed the slayings by an escaped prisoner at the Atlanta Fulton County Courthouse in March, but as authorities searched for the killer, something remarkable occurred.

ASHLEY SMITH AND BRIAN NICHOLS: PANCAKES AT DAWN

On Friday, March 11, defendant Brian Nichols was being escorted to his trial for rape and aggravated sodomy by a female deputy. When they reached the holding cell, the deputy uncuffed one of Nichols's hands, at which point the former college linebacker knocked her down, grabbed her gun, and beat her unconscious.

Although he could have simply escaped, Nichols instead crossed the bridge to the courthouse, where he hunted down, shot, and killed the judge in his case — Justice Roland Barnes — and the court reporter, Julie Brandau. He then ran back across the bridge and down a stairway to the street. On the way, he shot and killed Deputy Sheriff Hoyt Teasley, who had pursued him as he fled the building. Nichols then car-jacked a string of vehicles, murdering a customs agent named Rick Warren in the course of stealing his pickup truck later in the day.

Around 2 A.M. on March 12, Brian Nichols stuck a gun in the ribs of thirty-three-year-old Ashley Smith as she got out of her car in the parking lot of her apartment building. Nichols told her that if she screamed, he would kill her, but he added that if she would just do as he said, he would not hurt her. Smith assured him that she would do whatever he wanted. Nichols made her take him to her apartment, where he tied her up with electrical cords and duct tape.

Smith lost no time in beginning a conversation with her captor. She informed him that her husband had been stabbed to death four years earlier and had died in her arms. She said that if Nichols killed her, her five-year-old daughter wouldn't have a mommy or a daddy. She told Nichols that she was supposed to meet her daughter at church at 10 A.M. the next day and asked if he would let her go. He said no.

After searching the apartment and taking a shower, Nichols sat Smith down on her bed, and she asked if it would be all right if she read. When he said yes, she selected *The Purpose-Driven Life*,[1] and she began reading aloud where she'd last left off, at Day 33: "How Real Servants Act." Nichols asked her to repeat a passage, and they began discussing the role of purpose in their lives, which led to talk of God.

Smith later explained that she had been intent upon reaching out to Nichols at a human level, encouraging him to see her as a real person. Throughout their encounter, Smith talked about herself, her family, and things she had done, in an effort to establish a relationship with her captor. She repeated her request to be allowed to go and see her daughter Sunday morning, and Nichols's "no" gradually changed to "maybe" and "we'll see."

As they talked, Smith quietly exchanged the role of hostage for that of confidant. They discussed their faith, their families, and the massive manhunt going on outside. At some points they watched the coverage of the escape on television, and Nichols said that he could hardly believe that that was him they were talking about. Over the course of the night, Nichols untied Smith, and at his request, she showed him pictures of her daughter, as well as other family photos.

Eventually, Nichols asked Smith what she thought he ought to do. "If you don't turn yourself in," she replied, "lots more people are going to get hurt." Nichols called her "an angel" and his "sister in Christ," and he said God had led him to her door so that she'd tell him he had hurt a lot of people.

Ashley asked her captor if he believed in miracles. "You got out of that courthouse with police everywhere, and you don't think that's a miracle?" Smith demanded. "You don't think you're supposed to be sitting right here in front of me? Your miracle could be that you need to be caught for this. If you go to prison, then you need to share the word of God with all the prisoners there."

As Smith explained to reporters later: "He needed hope for his life. He said, 'Look at my eyes — I'm already dead.' I said: 'You're not dead! You're standing right in front of me! You're here in my apartment for some reason.'"

Before dawn, Nichols told Smith that he needed to ditch the pickup truck he'd stolen from the federal customs agent he'd murdered. Smith agreed to follow him in her car and to bring him back to her apartment after he dropped off the vehicle. Although it might have been possible for her to escape at this point, she said she followed through on her promise because she believed that if she abandoned him, he might have killed her and he would almost certainly have gone on to kill others. Besides, she had an idea that if she hung in there, she would be able to convince him to surrender.

Back at her apartment, Nichols quietly put his guns under her bed as if he were finished with them. He said that he'd rather have Smith shoot him than the people hunting him. Ashley Smith replied that she didn't want anyone to be hurt, not even him.

When morning came, Nichols was "overwhelmed" when Smith made him pancakes with real butter. He told her he "just wanted some normalness to his life."

Eventually he asked her, "What time do you have to go?" and Smith told him she had to meet her daughter at their church at ten o'clock, and so she would have to leave by 9:30. She thinks that by this point he understood and had accepted the fact that she would summon police, although nothing was said about it.

"He gave me some money when I was about to leave. Just kind of like he knew. I said, 'You might need this money.' And he said, 'No, I don't need it. I'm going to be here for the next few days.'"

Nichols asked if there was anything he could do for her while she was gone. She had just moved into the apartment two days earlier, and he offered to hang curtains for her. Significantly, before she left, he asked her to visit him in jail.

"I know he was probably hoping deep down that I was going to come back," Smith said, "but I think he knew what I had to do — that I had to turn him in."

Smith called 911 as soon as she got into her car. A SWAT team quickly surrounded her apartment building, and Nichols surrendered peacefully, waving a makeshift white flag.

The police were extremely impressed with Ashley Smith's handling of the situation. "She acted very cool and levelheaded," said Gwinnett County Police Officer Darren Moloney. "We don't normally see that in our profession. It was an absolutely best-case scenario that happened — a complete opposite of what you expected to happen. We were prepared for the worst and got the best."

"I believe God brought him to my door," Smith said afterward. When asked why she thought Nichols didn't kill her, she responded, "Because I didn't judge him."

Further Revelations

In late September 2005, Ashley Smith's personal account of this incident hit the bookstores, and some readers were shocked to learn that, at the time of these events, Smith was a drug addict. Although she initially didn't share this detail publicly, Smith admits in her book *Unlikely Angel: The Untold Story of the Atlanta Hostage Hero*[2] that when Nichols asked if she had any marijuana, she gave him her stash of crystal methamphetamine, but declined to join him in taking some.

"I chose not to do the drugs and he did," Smith explained. "It was a huge step for me because it was the first time I had said no to them."[3] She said, "If I did die, I wasn't going to heaven and say, 'Oh, excuse me, God. Let me wipe my nose, because I just did some drugs before I got here.'"[4]

In her book Smith says that she had lost custody of her daughter because of her addiction. However, she'd been working hard to turn her life around for months before her encounter with Brian Nichols. Further, having refused drugs that night, she says she has never had a desire to touch them since.

"It's hard for people to understand the miracle of the story," Ashley said when her book came out. "This was totally a God thing, to me in my life. This was God getting my attention, going, 'I'm going to give you one more chance.'"[5] At the time of the events, Ashley proclaimed, "My life is testimony that God can use us even in the midst of tragedy, and miracles do happen."[6]

Many in law enforcement and in the media also called Brian Nichols's peaceful surrender a "miracle." However, it's likely that most people used the word as hyperbole. When something really bad is about to happen, and then it doesn't, it's handy to say, "It's a miracle!" It doesn't necessarily mean the speaker really thinks that divine intervention was involved.

But I think it was.

I've been studying miracles for the past twenty-five years, and what I see that others may not is that *Ashley Smith did everything a person is supposed to do in order to make a miracle possible.* If you fulfill the necessary conditions for making divine intervention possible, and then something seemingly miraculous occurs, you have good reason to suppose that it isn't a mere coincidence.

Smith's extraordinarily skillful handling of Brian Nichols may seem absolutely unique, but I will show you many more instances where someone in grave danger did much the same thing, only to have a volatile situation end harmlessly. You see *there is a procedure for accessing miracles.* I believe that when we do our part, God, and enlightened beings acting on God's behalf, take care of the rest.

Could This Be a Miracle?

Admittedly, when we see Ashley Smith's story standing alone like this, there is no particular reason to suspect supernatural involvement. The same thing can be said of all of the narrow escapes we'll be exploring in this book. Taken individually, each of them appears to represent nothing more than a lucky break. Danger threatens, but things turn out all right. "Big deal!" some may cry. "Why should we drag in *miracles* to account for something that can be understood perfectly well without them?"

My case for miracles centers on the strange emotional

reactions displayed by people who experience narrow escapes. Like Ashley Smith, they all seem to slip into an extraordinarily peaceful, loving — even carefree — state of mind, behaving as though they were oblivious to danger. Of the people who described their experiences to me, not one said they thought of themselves as fearless or heroic, yet they amazed themselves with their sense of well-being while facing death.

This surprising equanimity reminded me of the peaceful detachment one experiences in meditation. I couldn't help wondering if perhaps these fortunate survivors had actually entered a meditative state. This idea was all the more intriguing because I was aware that going into meditation is precisely what spiritual traditions throughout the world say you ought to do if you want a miracle. Again and again, people reported that they had done the very thing mystics claim will make miracles possible, only to find a highly dangerous situation taking an unexpected turn for the better.

I believe that there is a technique for accessing miracles, and that anyone can learn to defuse life-threatening emergencies by doing just what Ashley Smith did. Let's look at another miracle story. As it happens, this story also involves a "Brian."

BRIAN: SHOWDOWN AT HIGH NOON

Brian had just received his doctorate in psychology and had been working at his first professional job in a maximum-security prison for only a few months when violence broke out. Prisoners seized weapons and hostages, occupied the library building, and began issuing nonnegotiable demands.

Tension mounted throughout the day as the National Guard arrived to surround the prison. Everyone waited breathlessly to hear the governor's response to the prisoners' demands.

Late in the afternoon, the warden stormed into Brian's office and shouted, "Goddamn it, you're the psychologist! You go in there and convince those prisoners to surrender!"

Brian could only conclude in retrospect that he must have been more afraid of his boss than of the rioting inmates. Minutes later, he found himself headed for the library to tell a group of armed and desperate murderers that the governor had rejected all of their demands and that they had just better throw down their weapons and release their hostages, or else!

"Or else what?!" Brian wondered, uncomfortably aware of what traditionally happens to the bearer of bad tidings. "Or else shoot me, I guess."

Brian was conscious of guns trained on him from every direction as he took that long walk across the yard. The silence was so profound that he could hear the blood pounding in his ears, and it seemed as though everyone in the prison was breathlessly waiting to see what would happen to him. Obviously, whatever occurred, Brian was going to be right in the middle. It seemed largely a matter of whether he would be shot accidentally by the guards or intentionally by the prisoners once the fireworks began.

Unable to see how he could have gotten himself into such a situation, Brian experienced a growing sense of unreality. A few minutes before, he had been a nice, middle-class young man trying to earn an honest living. Now, all of a sudden, he was Gary Cooper in *High Noon*. How, exactly, did something like this happen?

Despite his overwrought mental state — or possibly because of it — Brian found himself drifting into an amusing fantasy of himself playing this preposterous role in the best Hollywood tradition. He began to see himself as the Gary Cooper character in a Western — the lone figure of justice, warily moving down the empty main street of a frontier town. The prison guards became the townsfolk who watched from hiding as Brian went forth to fight their battle for them. That's right — Sheriff Brian, who would fearlessly confront odds that could only be beaten in a screenwriter's fantasy. Because a man's gotta do what a man's gotta do!

The next thing Brian knew, he had begun to parody himself and his absurd fantasy. Pausing dramatically, he squared off against the library, hands flexing over imaginary six-shooters on his hips. He began to stalk toward the building in a ridiculous burlesque of the classic gunfighter swagger. Feeling the need for a little musical accompaniment, he shattered the tense silence by loudly whistling "Do Not Forsake Me, Oh My Darling," the theme from *High Noon*.

For a few moments, guards and prisoners watched Brian's bizarre performance in stunned silence. Then they began getting it. Brian as Gary Cooper. People acting as if this goofy kid was going to be able to face down a gang of armed killers. Suddenly everyone could see how absurd the situation had become.

Laughter rang out from all sides. Fed by the tension that had been building all day, it rose to hysterical heights. Guards and prisoners alike became helpless with hilarity as their anxiety poured out of them in foot-stomping, knee-pounding guffaws. People laughed until they cried — until they could barely stand up.

When it was over, Brian strolled into the library and explained the governor's response and the hopelessness of their position to the prisoners, who by now regarded him as a hell of a guy. Minutes later, he presided over their peaceful surrender.

WHAT ARE MIRACLES?

If I'm to make a case for the idea that Ashley and Brian both created miracles, it might be well to begin by clarifying what I mean by that. Author C. S. Lewis defined a *miracle* as *an instance in which a supernatural power interferes in the natural world*, and this is the definition I will be using here.[7] But notice that this is not an *operational* definition of the type required for scientific inquiry. It captures the essence of what we mean when we call something a miracle, but doesn't specify exactly what observations or measurements would allow one to determine whether an event is miraculous or natural. I believe it is impossible to specify such things, since what truly allows us to differentiate a miracle from a piece of good luck is not anything inherent in the event itself, but rather the inner process of the person experiencing it.

Some investigators try to solve the problem of identifying which events result from divine intervention by confining their attention to experiences so extraordinary and inexplicable that it seems they *could not* have been caused by any known or suspected natural means and *must* therefore have been caused by the power of God, possibly acting through an intermediary such as an angel, prophet, saint, or healer. For example, if the Red Sea suddenly parted when Moses stretched his rod out over it, or a body that was well and truly dead was resurrected from its tomb three days later, it's hard to see how there could be any "perfectly ordinary" explanation for what occurred. Skeptics can argue that such things never really happened, but if they did happen, they certainly seem like the work of a supernatural power.

One problem with this approach is that wonders of this magnitude do not really lend themselves to verification. First of all, if we call an event "miraculous" only in those rare instances where we believe we can *conclusively* rule out every possible cause except a supernatural one, we'll be confining our attention to a set of circumstances so singular that most of us will never have any firsthand experience with it. And can we ever really be sure that whoever undertook to investigate the incident actually did rule out *every* other possibility? The evidence will only seem "conclusive" to the extent that we credit a stranger's story about what happened. Take, for example, this account by my friend Hayden and her mother, Doris, of a purportedly miraculous rescue during a family trip to the beach.

HAYDEN AND DORIS: THE MAN WHO WASN'T THERE

When Hayden was twelve years old, her family went on a vacation to Daytona Beach, Florida. On this particular day, Hayden's father had gone into town for an hour or so, leaving the little girl and her mother, Doris, to enjoy the off-season luxury of an enormous stretch of deserted sand and sea. Doris paddled around in an inner tube while Hayden held onto the outside. The two chatted contentedly, savoring the delightful contrast of cool water and hot sunshine.

Hayden thinks that they must somehow have lost all track of time because the water suddenly got rough. Looking up, the pair was startled to realize that they had drifted far out to sea. The beach was just a line on the horizon, and the wind was carrying them out into the shipping lanes at a high rate of speed. The next thing they knew, several large swells washed over them from out of nowhere. Hayden was torn away from the inner tube and swamped by the waves.

A poor swimmer to begin with, the twelve-year-old struggled to the surface and fought to get back to her mother and the safety of the tube. Doris was frantically trying to reach her as well, but despite their best efforts, the distance between them just kept widening. Now thrashing around in panic, Hayden began to drown. Wave after wave rolled over her. She was dragged repeatedly beneath the choking surface, only to struggle weakly back into the air.

Finally, exhausted by her unequal contest with the sea, Hayden knew that she couldn't go on. Her panic went away, and she found herself strangely at peace with the prospect of dying. As she was about to stop her useless struggles and let the waves take her under, a man appeared in the water a few feet away. Although there had been no one in sight the whole time they'd been at the beach, here suddenly was a strong swimmer right next to her!

Doris and Hayden agree that the man was dark haired and seemed to be in his thirties, although they didn't have time to notice much else or wonder where he'd come from. Hayden lunged for his outstretched hand, but she couldn't quite reach it. Since she'd missed it by only an inch or so, she gathered her flagging strength and tried again. Again she missed, but only just.

"What I didn't realize," Hayden told me, "is that he was actually towing both of us to shore. Mother and I were trying as hard as we could to reach the guy, and he was somehow pulling us with him while staying just beyond reach. Although we'd been way out in the ocean, and although we never could quite reach his outstretched hand, we were moving toward the beach. And quickly, too! I suddenly looked up and found myself in shallow water quite close to the shore. At that point the man gently gathered me up in his arms and carried me the rest of the way up onto the beach.

"He lowered me to the sand, and I immediately began to vomit up the water I'd swallowed. Mother ran up onto the beach right behind us, and she fell to her knees beside me and held me as I retched."

Both women think that it took Hayden about a minute to vomit up the water she had swallowed. Then the two of them settled back on the sand and looked around to thank their rescuer. But there was no one there.

"And I mean no one!" Hayden emphasizes. "Just as before, the beach and the water were empty as far as the eye could see. And the eye could see clearly for a good half mile in every direction!

"You've got to understand that this was a totally flat and featureless beach flanked on one side by a flat, calm ocean and on the other by a deserted parking lot. I wasn't vomiting more than a minute at the most, and an Olympic sprinter couldn't have gotten out of sight in that amount of time. There was simply nowhere he could have gone.

"Mother and I are both certain that there had been no one anywhere near us before I started drowning, and it was clear that there was no one anywhere near us now. The man had appeared out of thin air and then vanished back into it. He somehow towed both of us to shore against the wind and the current without touching either of us, carried me out of the water, and then simply dematerialized.

"I'm sure that some people would say we were just distracted and confused, but we both saw what happened and we both know beyond any possibility of mistake that this was not an ordinary human being. Mother and I both believe that we were rescued by an angel."

Given the prevalence of reports about angels rescuing humans, I think that an unbiased individual must at least consider the possibility that such things really happen. Nevertheless, it's clear that they don't happen every day. And unless they happen to you, how do you know what to believe?

If this rescue really occurred the way Hayden and Doris say it did, then it certainly seems as if some supernatural power intervened on their behalf. How could an ordinary human being materialize and dematerialize? If they were mistaken in thinking that he did this, we are still left to explain how an ordinary man could have towed them both to shore without physical contact. And if he were only a hallucination and they really swam in under their own power, who lifted Hayden out of the water and carried her up onto the beach?

It's also difficult to see how the impression of these events could have resulted from either mental confusion or an honest mistake. If they had been experienced by only one person, we might write them off as an aberration induced by stress. But both Hayden and Doris agree that they saw the same things. And while we psychologists sometimes toss around terms such as *group hallucination* to account for inexplicable events witnessed by more than one person, the term has no real explanatory value. Psychology knows of no mechanism that can explain how two or more people could hallucinate the same thing at the same time.

The simplest explanation is, of course, that they are both lying. However, I know these women personally, and to me the idea that they would make up such a story and stick to it all these years seems no less incredible than the possibility that they were really rescued by an angel. Of course, you don't know them, so what convinces me may not convince you.

And that's precisely my point. If the argument for miracles rests upon tales of impossible occurrences told by strangers, it will never be truly convincing. Who knows whether the witnesses are at all credible? And even if they are, how far does that take us?

Most people today are aware of the inherent limitations of eyewitness testimony. Even jurors watching a crime enacted before them on videotape often can't agree about what they're seeing, despite an opportunity to review the material dozens of times. If that is so, then how much confidence can we place in the eyewitness testimony of strangers who claim to have experienced divine intervention? However convincingly miraculous this aquatic rescue may have seemed to

Hayden and Doris, those of us who hear of it at second hand are entitled to be skeptical.

Even the best scientific research on miracles involves this same limitation. For example, there is an International Medical Commission that has been studying miraculous healings associated with the Shrine of the Virgin at Lourdes, France, since the 1940s. At this point, sixty-five cases out of the thousands of reported cures have survived rigorous investigation and been declared miraculous by the Catholic Church.[8]

However, the commission's conclusions still leave you and me in the position of having to take someone else's word for what happened. Scientists have biases and make mistakes just like the rest of us. And there will always be equally qualified authorities arguing for the other side of any really interesting question. Even if we are prepared to accept what "experts" have to say about miracles, how are we to decide which experts to believe?

BELIEVING THE IMPROBABLE

But the study of miracles need not revolve around impossible wonders that happen to others. If there really is a supernatural power that intervenes to heal and rescue humans, it seems unlikely that its activities would be confined to situations outside the realm of everyday human experience. Once we know what to look for, I think we'll find smaller, "garden-variety" miracles blooming in our own backyards, where we can look at them up close and form our own opinions about the way they work.

These *surprising* but by no means *unbelievable* reversals

of fortune cannot be identified as miracles through their apparent impossibility. Nevertheless, I think you'll see that before each one occurs, the individual experiencing it does something rather extraordinary. In the face of grave danger, she or he releases judgment and emotional conflict to retreat into a detached and loving state of mind some might call "beatific" or "fully surrendered." It is this surprising shift in consciousness we'll be using to distinguish actual miracles from ordinary lucky breaks.

I believe in miracles because I've experienced them. I figure that when you experience them, you'll believe in them, too.

Things to Think About

1) Miracles may be found in situations where a positive outcome is surprising, but by no means impossible. Can you think of any such instances from your own life or the lives of people you know well?

2) Individuals who experience miracles seem to first enter a peaceful altered state of the kind traditionally associated with meditation. Have you ever meditated?

3) Miracles may already have happened to you, or to people you know, without anyone having recognized them as such.

Chapter Two

Discovering Miracles of Deliverance

[Zen meditation] is a heightened state
of concentrated awareness wherein one is neither
tense nor hurried, and certainly never slack.
It is the mind of somebody facing death.

— *Yasutani Roshi*

I am an experimental psychologist by training. I received a
PhD in experimental psychology in 1978 with a specialization in motivation and emotion. In the course of some twenty
years teaching psychology, I supervised numerous dissertations and theses, and I published on a wide range of topics,
from classical conditioning to the creation of a test for a sense
of humor. I became a licensed clinical psychologist in 1984
and have been in independent practice ever since. How, you
might ask, does someone with that sort of academic background come to be studying miracles?

My interest in the subject began with my own narrow
escape from what looked like certain death. Here's what

happened. I was driving up to the mountains near Los Angeles to enjoy the winter weather. The air in the city was balmy, but as I climbed the Angeles Crest Highway, it got colder. Patches of snow began to appear, and I got out to make snowballs and savor the season.

Back on the road, I rounded a tight curve when I heard a bang and the car suddenly went out of control. Though I didn't piece it together until afterward, one of my rear tires blew out just as I was crossing a patch of black ice. I must have been going thirty-five or forty miles per hour.

The car went wild. I was briefly grateful for the fact that there was no one coming from the opposite direction as I skidded across the other lane. However, it was soon clear that my gratitude was premature. Beyond the lane for oncoming traffic was a narrow scenic overlook area. And beyond that was the edge of a cliff. I was now hurtling sideways across the deserted parking area on a trajectory that would inevitably take my car over the brink.

It's hard to explain what happened next, especially since it's difficult to see how there could have been time for all the thoughts and reactions I experienced. All I can say is that time seemed to expand.

First, although I don't think of myself as a brave person, I wasn't at all frightened. The magnitude of the danger actually seemed to place me beyond fear. What point was there in being afraid once the worst was inevitable? Concern about my safety gave way before a need to prepare for my death.

I remember being surprised by the fact that I was about to die. Hoping that I was mistaken, I looked the situation over again, but it was clear that I had more than enough momentum to skid over the edge.

"Gee, wouldn't you think you'd know it if you were about to die?" I mused. "It's clear that no one survives a fall like this, but even now I don't feel as though I'm going to die. But maybe everyone feels surprise and no one has any idea that they're going to die before they actually do. Still, you'd think you'd know at some level."

I wondered what dying was going to be like. Maybe I would suffer. Maybe the car would burst into flames the way cars do in movies when they go over cliffs. But then I thought, "It won't matter. I'll be out of my body by then." And another part piped up with, "Oh yeah! Like you know all about it."

I vaguely regretted the fact that I had to die now. I wished that there were something I could do to get out of it. And then another part of my mind said, "Well, why don't you see if there is?"

So I searched my memory to see if there was anything I knew that might be useful. But all I could come up with was the idea that when you are skidding, you are supposed to steer into the skid. Had I read that in the manual for the driving test? I wasn't sure of the source, but I did recall that that was what experts say to do.

"Well, that's no use here," I told myself. "I'm already really close to the edge. If I turn the wheels in that direction, I'll just go over sooner."

But then I thought, "Well, what have I got to lose by trying? It's not as though I have a lot of options here." So I figured, "What the hell" and turned the wheel into the skid.

By now I was practically at the edge. I figured that if there were any chance at all, I would have to steer into the skid until the last possible moment and then turn the wheel away from the precipice. And when I turned, it would have to be fast, but not too fast or I would skid again. How would I recognize the ultimate moment when turning would still be possible? It was probably already too late.

I became incredibly focused upon the feel of the car and the sight of the approaching cliff. It was as if the whole world had narrowed to this one problem. I was perfectly calm, as though it were some sort of totally absorbing intellectual exercise, figuring out just when and how to turn the wheel. And all the time I was watching myself with a sense of irony, since it clearly wasn't going to make any difference what I did. Not even a professional stunt driver could pull this one off!

I sat there steering toward the cliff for what seemed like a very long time as the brink approached in slow motion. The ground had actually disappeared from view in front of me before a voice in my head said, "Now!"

At this signal, I turned the wheel smoothly to the right — fast, but not too fast. And to my astonishment, the car followed the wheel. I was out of the skid, and I swept gracefully away from the brink and back across the highway. With most of its momentum now exhausted, my car ran up on some boulders at the base of the cliff on the other side, and it was over.

I got out to survey the damage. The front bumper was a little bent where I had run up on the rocks, and of course, my tire was flat, but otherwise the car was fine. Then I crossed the highway and looked at the skid marks in the dirt. The distance between the road and the edge of the cliff was about thirty feet. At the point where I had turned, the tire marks came to within three feet of the brink.

How long did it take my car to skid to the edge of the cliff? A car going thirty miles per hour covers forty-four feet per second. If I started the skid at about thirty-five miles per hour and the edge was some thirty feet away, it cannot realistically have taken much more than a second. Yet it was the longest second of my life. I felt as though I had all the time in the world to think things out, make decisions, and execute them.

A few moments later, vehicles appeared from both directions and pulled over to help. Two men dragged my car off the rocks and whipped on my spare tire. Within minutes, I was starting for home as though nothing had happened.

When I thought about the incident on the way back to Los Angeles, I was awed to think of the driving maneuver that I had pulled off. I also recognized that I could never have hoped to do it in ordinary consciousness. There was something about my oddly peaceful altered state that allowed me to put total concentration into my driving. Combined with the slow-motion effect, it permitted me to calculate my reactions to a fraction of a second.

The fearlessness I'd experienced in that state had also been critical. If I had been afraid as I approached the edge, I could not have thought clearly or held the car on course as long as was needed, and I would inevitably have skidded over the cliff. And then there was that voice in my head that seemed to coach me through the accident.

Still puzzling over this incident, I mentioned it a few days later to my friend and spiritual teacher Carmela Corallo. "Now that's funny," she replied. "I had an experience just like that this week." Here's what happened to Carmela two days after my accident.

CARMELA: RISING TO THE OCCASION

Carmela was strolling with her friend Fred on the bluffs near her home in Encinitas, California. It was a perfect day, and the path offered a spectacular view of the surf pounding on the rocks far below. When they came to a smaller path that snaked down the face of the bluff, Fred suggested they climb down it, and Carmela readily agreed.

"Now, I knew better than to do that. Every year there are news stories about people who are killed climbing on the bluffs. The ground is very unstable, and pieces are always falling away into the ocean. There are signs everywhere warning people to stay away from the edge, but I guess I've seen them so many times I don't even notice them anymore.

"Anyway, we started climbing down the path. It was so narrow that we had to walk in single file, and Fred led the way. We came to a place where it turned back up, and we were headed back to the top when the path suddenly fell away between the places Fred and I were standing. Then the path gave way behind me. I was perched on a little patch of ground that obviously wasn't going to be there for long either. I could hear the fallen earth crashing onto the rocks below, and I remember thinking, 'Boy, was this ever a bad idea!'

"It should have been a frightening situation, but strangely enough, it wasn't. I found myself becoming completely calm. I realized that I had done a very foolish thing in coming down here, but it still seemed to me that everything would be all right. I went into meditation immediately and asked for help."

Carmela was then a woman in her forties, and although she was in good physical shape, she'd never thought of herself as much of an athlete. Fred, who had scrambled up the path ahead, shouted encouragement and suggestions from above, but there was no way he could reach her or help directly. It seemed obvious that she could not go on standing where she was, so she instantly began climbing straight up.

"I reached up and found a toehold and a couple of handholds. As soon as I lifted my weight off of the patch of path, it dropped into the ocean, too. Now there was no alternative but to keep going.

"The whole climb was like that. Every time I moved my weight off a place, it crumbled and fell. Every toehold held just as long as I needed it to and not a moment longer. I just kept moving."

Carmela reported that she actually felt quite cheerful as she worked her way up the nearly vertical face of the bluff. "It was an adventure — a challenge. I was totally absorbed in the task at hand, constantly scanning for places to get a hold on the cliff. Somehow, there always seemed to be another one just within reach. I never let it enter my mind that I might reach a place where I couldn't go any farther, or that I might fall onto the rocks. I wasn't afraid to die, but I didn't want to, so I just pushed that possibility right out of existence.

I asked for divine help and trusted that I would be shown what to do. And I was.

"Fred raced up to the top of the bluff and was there to get a hold of me and pull me the rest of the way as I scrambled over the edge. We clung to each other and laughed with relief when it was over."

I was deeply impressed by the fact that Carmela had had such a similar experience within a few days of mine. She, too, had been in danger of falling over a cliff to what seemed like certain death. She, too, had entered a peaceful, fearless, intensely focused state of consciousness and then discovered skills and abilities she had not known she possessed. Some higher aspect of her own consciousness had seemed to watch over and guide her, too. The coincidence was so striking that I couldn't help thinking that it must mean something. But what?

Still working over these incidents in my mind, I mentioned them in one of my classes in the graduate program where I was teaching psychology. A student named Karen came up to me after the lecture and remarked in a confidential undertone, "Oh, by the way, Carolyn. It would still have been all right, even if you'd gone off the cliff. That's what happened to me." Intrigued, I asked for details. She related the following story.

KAREN AND MIKE: BEAVERS TO THE RESCUE

Karen had gone with her boyfriend, Mike, to visit her family in the mountains of Colorado. Since the road to the house was poorly marked, Karen's brother met them at a nearby town so that he could lead the way. It was late at night before they started up the mountain.

Familiar with the road, Karen's brother drove quickly and confidently. Mike often saw his taillights disappear into the darkness ahead and had to hurry to keep from losing him altogether. As a result, he was going too fast to negotiate a tight turn that seemed to appear out of nowhere. In a moment, Mike was driving straight over the side of the mountain, and he and Karen were plunging into the darkness below.

Karen remembers feeling relaxed and amused as they sailed over the side. On the one hand, she knew that people who drive off cliffs in the Rocky Mountains don't live very long, but on the other, she had the irrational conviction that everything was going to be just fine. She found herself in an altered state of consciousness that was serene and even whimsical, and she said Mike reported having a very similar experience.

Time seemed to expand, and many thoughts drifted lazily through Karen's head. "Well," she reflected ironically, "I guess this is why they tell you to wear seat belts!" Karen realized that neither she nor Mike was wearing one, but this thought was quickly followed by the conviction that it couldn't possibly matter with a fall of this magnitude. Yet, despite the fact that logic told her she and Mike were about to die, she was absolutely confident that everything would turn out fine.

Strangely enough, it did. The car splashed down in the middle of a beaver pond just deep enough to break its fall.

Once the waves subsided, Karen and Mike discovered that the water came to just below the windows. As cold trickles began to leak in through the doors, the two climbed onto the roof, where they huddled together, laughing and singing songs to pass the time.

Soon a motorist noticed their skid marks going over the edge and stopped to see what had happened. The two hailed him boisterously as he peered down into the darkness, and he went for help. Before long the car was towed out of the pond. It was undamaged and started up without difficulty.

The local people who gathered at the scene of the accident were doubly amazed. First, it was hard for them to believe that Karen and Mike and their car had come through such a spectacular fall without so much as a scratch. But there was a further source of wonder. Although they passed the spot daily, none of them had ever seen a beaver pond there before.

The juxtaposition of these three highly unusual, yet strikingly similar, incidents made a strong impression on me. They seemed somehow to be cut from the same cloth. When I began mentioning them to other groups and classes, I found that often someone would chime in and say, "That's just like what happened to me!" And sure enough it was. I learned that a great many people had faced what appeared to be serious danger only to go into a curiously peaceful altered state of consciousness and discover that things worked out fine.

Sometimes, as in my case or Carmela's, the positive outcome seemed to depend upon the skillful way in which the person was inspired to handle the emergency. Other cases followed the pattern of Karen and Mike's accident, where the individuals involved could do nothing but rest in a peaceful state and await developments. Some attributed spiritual significance to their deliverance, while others never considered the possibility that it was anything more than incredibly good luck.

Yet in every story, the persons involved were astonished by the strangely peaceful, fearless altered state in which they'd found themselves. Some described it as having a humorous quality, while others felt total self-confidence, boundless compassion, or a sense of being guided and protected by some benevolent higher power. A number reported the experience of time expanding, and many agreed that they had somehow known that everything was going to be all right whatever was to happen. In a few cases, fear or anger was an alternative consciousness that seemed to compete for attention with the sense of peace, but for most, fear was conspicuous by its absence.

As intriguing as I found these stories, I don't believe I would have recognized their underlying significance if I had not been a student of spirituality as well as a psychologist. On the one hand, I was learning about various mystical thought systems, especially the one found in *A Course in Miracles*.[1] On the other, I was being inundated with the true stories of ordinary people who survived life-threatening situations after spontaneously following the very procedure these traditions recommend in order to create miracles. I couldn't help wondering if these could have been actual instances of divine intervention.

Let me take a moment here to say a few words about *A Course in Miracles*, since it informs everything I write about miracles in this book. The *Course* is a three-volume set of books ("Text," "Lessons for Students," and a "Manual for Teachers"). It was purportedly channeled from Jesus Christ in the 1960s by two psychologists, Drs. Helen Schucman and William Thetford, who were colleagues at Columbia Presbyterian Medical Center in New York City. A nonprofit organization called The Foundation for Inner Peace was set up to publish the *Course* anonymously. In accord with Jesus's instructions, the *Course* was never to be advertised, and it was to be sold at cost or given away free to anyone who couldn't afford to pay for it. As of this writing, the *Course* has been translated into eleven languages other than English, with ten more translations in progress. A nondenominational approach to spiritual awakening, the *Course* outlines a "universal curriculum" common to all religions. It provides the most lucid explanation of miracles, inner guidance, and the path to spiritual liberation that I've ever encountered.[2]

WHO EXPERIENCES MIRACLES?

At this point, about 70 percent of the people who have shared their stories with me have been psychotherapists. This is because I collected most of these accounts informally during the years I worked as a psychologist in academia, so the people I came in contact with tended to be in the same field. Many were students in my graduate-level psychology classes; some were colleagues who contacted me to contribute their own stories after hearing of my preliminary findings at professional conferences; and still other contributors were readers of the 1995 edition of *Creating Miracles*, who then sent their own miracle stories to me.

I believe it is significant that many of my informants have tended to be spiritually oriented individuals. While most are not conventionally religious, in every case in which the person's attitude toward spiritual matters is known to me, he or she has turned out to have participated in some spiritual or quasi-spiritual practice. Many have attended twelve-step programs or studied meditation, yoga, martial arts, or shamanism; several considered a religious vocation at some point in their lives. As we shall see, centering the mind in peace appears to be essential for obtaining a miracle. While this is an ability everyone possesses, it is probable that this comes more easily to people who have already practiced some form of prayer, contemplation, or meditation.

On the other hand, whether they were spiritual-minded or not, none of the people who shared their stories with me were candidates for sainthood. I'm convinced that the commonly held belief that God helps the "good" while leaving "sinners" to fend for themselves is completely misguided. The most ordinary of people can confidently expect to receive miracles when they sincerely open up to them. That goes for drug addicts like Ashley Smith and criminals like Brian Nichols as well as for atheists and agnostics. Nor are miracles reserved for the members of any particular faith. Divine help and guidance are reported all over the world, and it is clear that no spiritual tradition has an exclusive contract with God.

Things to Think About

1) Have you ever noticed the way things work more smoothly when you're in a good mood than they do when you are in a bad one? Or the way everyone is so friendly and helpful to you when you're in love? These are examples of the way your state of consciousness influences the kind of experiences you attract.

2) What have you been taught about miracles? Are these teachings consistent with what I've been saying here?

3) Have you ever imagined yourself unworthy of God's help? Remember, a loving parent wants the best for all of her or his children, and will go to extraordinary lengths to guide and assist those who have lost their way.

Chapter Three

But Doesn't Science Deny the Possibility of Miracles?

Science without religion is lame,
religion without science is blind.

— *Albert Einstein*

*T*he very idea of taking miracles seriously may strike some as absurd due to a widespread misconception that science has already proven that miracles *cannot* exist. Since this confusion is common, let's look at it before we go any further. After all, if reports of miracles are nothing more than pleasing fantasies, like stories about unicorns and perpetual-motion machines, why waste our time on them?

I've said that miracles are "instances where a supernatural power interferes with nature." Belief in their impossibility results, not from science itself, but from a particular philosophy of science called *naturalism* that was in vogue from the late nineteenth century into the first half of the

twentieth century. Naturalists defined "nature" as "the total-
ity of that which exists."

Now, it goes without saying that if we start from the assumption that everything that exists is part of nature, there
can be nothing "supernatural." Under this theory, everything
real is rendered "natural" *by definition*. Religious people, in
contrast, usually accept instead some form of *supernaturalism*.
Some supernaturalists hold that there are two kinds of things
that exist in the universe. In addition to nature (creation),
there is also an original, self-existing entity that created nature and that continues to exist beyond time and space (God).
An alternate form of supernaturalism agrees with naturalism that there is only one substance in the universe, but it
says that that substance is ultimately divine rather than
purely physical.

If naturalism is true, then what appear to be miracles must
really be caused by as-yet-undiscovered natural processes; they
certainly do not constitute credible evidence of the existence
of a Supreme Being with loving intentions toward humans.
But is this true? To find out, we must decide whether naturalism provides a convincing and realistic account of the
world we experience.

THE NATURALIST VIEW

Because naturalism holds that only physical things are real, it
denies existence to anything that cannot be perceived with the
five senses, or with instruments such as microscopes and tele-
scopes that expand the reach of the senses. It is also a deter-
ministic philosophy: it assumes that everything that happens

must happen because it is part of a pattern set in motion at the dawn of time. It denies not only the possibility of supernatural events like miracles but also the reality of familiar phenomena such as thoughts, minds, love, and free will. Although we humans have the subjective impression that we are choosing what to do in each situation, naturalists believe that we are really just behaving as our bodies and brains have been programmed to do by our individual genetic makeup and our histories of reinforcement and punishment.

This implies that we are not morally responsible for our actions. For example, the influential behavioral scientist B. F. Skinner argued that we shouldn't praise or blame people for the things they do because they have no real choice in the matter.[1] If naturalism is correct, we are all simply automatons. Skinner is best known for his role in developing a form of psychology called Radical Behaviorism that does not acknowledge the existence of the *psyche* or mind.

As you can already see, you don't need to believe in God or the supernatural to disagree with naturalism. Indeed, nearly all contemporary scientists have abandoned the idea that only physical things are real, and Skinner's Radical Behaviorism has since given birth to Cognitive Behaviorism, a theory that explicitly acknowledges the importance of nonmaterial things such as thoughts, beliefs, and emotions, as well as their impact on the physical systems of the body and brain.

Most modern researchers fully embrace the idea that mind and free will do exist, and as we shall see, some physicists are even encountering an invisible, causal dimension of the universe that is accurately characterized as "supernatural," in that it stands outside of nature and is not constrained by natural laws as we presently understand them. As attractive as naturalism once was to scientists, they have had to give it up in order to come to terms with the actual complexity of things.

So, while it's true that some scientists continue to dismiss supernatural phenomena, and that the existence of miracles is not likely ever to be scientifically verified, that doesn't mean they aren't real — or indeed that people who respect science don't believe in them. For example, one 2005 study[2] found that 76 percent of physicians in the United States say they believe in God, and 59 percent believe in an afterlife.

In the past century, the dogmatic rejection of the very possibility of supernatural phenomena has lost much of its appeal for intellectuals. As the distinguished physicist Charles Townes, who co-invented the laser and shared the 1964 Nobel Prize for physics for his work in quantum electronics, recently put it:

> If you look at what religion is all about, it's trying to understand the purpose and meaning of our universe. Science tries to understand function and structures. In the long run they must come together. Their differences are largely superficial, and the two become almost indistinguishable if we look at the real nature of each.[3]

INVESTIGATING MIRACLES SCIENTIFICALLY

All scientists agree — no matter what their point of view or beliefs about the supernatural — that events in the physical universe appear to be governed by natural laws, and the scientific study of those laws follows agreed-upon practices. However, to study nonphysical phenomena, you can't simply apply the scientific methods designed to measure the physical world. Yardsticks and chemical analyses are of limited usefulness when it comes to identifying the presence or absence of a miracle.

Nevertheless, even supposing we could overcome the problem of creating experiments that operationalized the important variables, most people wouldn't change their most deeply held convictions on the basis of a single scientific study, or even a series of such studies. And this is as true of scientists as it is of laypeople. When research results fail to support a particular theory, those who believe in the theory don't just shrug their shoulders and change their minds. Nor should they.

Scientists know that there are numerous ways an experiment can fail to support a true hypothesis — inaccurate measurements, inadequate controls, contamination, fraud, and poorly defined variables, to name but a few. Consequently, when research doesn't yield the expected results, scientists continue trying to design better studies in an effort to find experimental support for what they believe to be true. Of course, most scientists whose expectations are constantly confounded will eventually give up their theory. But how much negative evidence is "enough" varies depending upon the scientist and the strength of her or his original conviction.

The upshot is that even when the authenticity of allegedly supernatural events is investigated by credible experts, their findings are not necessarily the last word on the subject. Science progresses by constantly reevaluating and expanding upon currently accepted wisdom. Today's "scientifically proven fact" is often tomorrow's "popular misconception," and theories like relativity and evolution, which seemed absurd to one generation of scientists, sometimes find abundant support in the work of the next. To show you what I mean, consider the efforts to authenticate the Shroud of Turin.

The Shroud of Turin

The Shroud is a 14-by-3.5-foot length of linen that many believe bears the miraculous image of the crucified Christ. The Shroud turned up in France in 1355, when it was donated to the Catholic Church by a knight named Geoffroy de Charney, who claimed it was the grave cloth of Jesus, imprinted with his likeness during the process of resurrection. De Charney was unwilling to say how the Shroud had come into his possession, and the Catholic Church has never asserted its authenticity.

Many historians regard the Shroud as a fake produced in Europe in medieval times, either to inspire faith or to enrich the perpetrators of the hoax.[4] They point, first of all, to the Shroud's dubious provenance. If it was authentic, where had it been for fourteen and a half centuries, and why wouldn't de Charney say where he'd gotten it?

These objections certainly raise serious doubts about the relic's authenticity, but here's one possible explanation, endorsed by some, albeit by no means all, investigators. An ancient tradition in the Eastern Orthodox Church holds that Jesus's Shroud was taken to Turkey after the resurrection.

However, as a grave cloth it was ritually unclean according to Jewish law. We must remember that for the first several hundred years of the common era, the followers of Christ considered themselves Jews. This meant that the Shroud was not only one of the early Christians' holiest relics, it was also taboo — an item they were forbidden even to touch.

Some historians believe that to disguise the Shroud's "unclean" origin and make it possible to display the image it bore within a sacred space, the followers of Christ in Turkey may have folded it in such a way as to show only Jesus's head. It is known that for many centuries an allegedly miraculous likeness of Jesus's face called the "Edessan Image" was displayed in a Turkish church before disappearing during the chaos of the Crusades.

Some historians speculate that the Shroud may have been seized from the Eastern Orthodox Church by the Knights Templar when Constantinople was looted by Crusaders in 1204. If it is true that the Shroud had been in the possession of the Templars, there's no real mystery about de Charney's reluctance to discuss his acquisition of it. No French knight in 1355 would have dared identify himself to authorities of the Catholic Church as having any connection with the Templars, given that in 1307 the Pope had ordered the arrest, torture, and execution of all of the members of that order. Thus, the transfer of the Shroud, by some surviving Templar or his descendant, to representatives of the Catholic Church was likely to have been an early instance of "don't ask, don't tell."

In 1898 the Shroud was first photographed and the image on it was found to have the properties of a photographic negative, certainly an odd thing for medieval forgers to have faked. Since then, skeptics have come up with any number of plausible explanations to account for the Shroud's manufacture and the peculiar properties of the image it bears. However, as each theory explaining how the image could have been produced by an artist has been demonstrated, new evidence for the Shroud's authenticity has soon followed. One year the doubters seem to have definitively proven, for example, that the image was produced by brushing paint over a low-relief sculpture, or formed in a camera obscura in an early experiment with photography. The next year, the tide of evidence once again favors believers.

Results from the Shroud of Turin Research Project in the 1970s indicated that upon chemical analysis, what had appeared to be blood stains actually showed signs of red ochre and vermillion pigments, indicating that they had been produced with tempera paint.[5] And when a sample of the cloth was divided into three small portions and sent to three different laboratories for radiocarbon dating in 1978, all of the labs agreed that it was produced between 1260 and 1390 CE.[6] The matter seemed settled. The Shroud was definitely a fraud.

But wait! Other scientists came up with alternative explanations for the carbon dating findings. It was noted that the part of the Shroud that was tested came from an area that had received a lot of handling, and was therefore highly contaminated by dirt, bacteria, and slime mold, any one of which could have contributed to a carbon date much nearer the present. And still other researchers found pollen on the Shroud that could only have been acquired in Jerusalem, as well as some indicative of a prolonged stay in Turkey. The composition and weave of the cloth was found to be essentially identical to linen known to have been produced in Jerusalem and conclusively dated to the period of the crucifixion. More sophisticated chemical analysis revealed that the apparent bloodstains — far from being paint — were, in fact, made by real human blood.

In 2003, Raymond N. Rogers, a retired chemist from Los Alamos National Laboratory and one of the original researchers involved with the carbon dating of the Shroud, was given several threads of the Shroud to analyze. He determined, first of all, that these threads — which had been taken from the interior of the Shroud — were completely dissimilar to the ones taken from the edge that had been analyzed by the Shroud of Turin Project. It is now believed that the cloth at the edges had been attached during the medieval period in an effort to preserve and repair the unraveling fibers of the original.

Rogers then analyzed the interior threads for vanillin content. Vanillin is present in the flax from which linen is made, and like carbon 14, it disappears at a known rate over time. Rogers found that the Shroud's original threads no longer contained any vanillin, which led him to conclude that the Shroud could be as much as three thousand years old. If the cloth dated from the Middle Ages, it should have had 37 percent of its vanillin remaining.[7]

Will the current crop of studies settle the Shroud's date and place of origin once and for all? Don't bet on it. The ball is now in the skeptics' court, and I confidently expect it to be returned over the net in the near future. The reality is that scientific conclusions are always tentative. New research continually alters our understanding, and science must constantly change to keep pace with new discoveries.

But even if every scientist is eventually compelled to agree that the Shroud was produced in Jerusalem around the time of the crucifixion, how do we know it wasn't faked then? No amount of research is going to conclusively prove that the image on the Shroud was created by a burst of radiation associated with Jesus's resurrection. The most that could be said is that the evidence is consistent with that possibility, and that isn't going to change the mind of anyone predisposed to doubt.

The fact is that science seldom convinces anyone to change their fundamental beliefs. Researchers on both sides of an argument will keep searching for and finding evidence to support their existing points of view. Even if you were prepared to change your beliefs on the basis of scientific evidence, how would you know when to settle for the current crop? Or do you just continually change back and forth with each new research advance?

Bias in Scientific Research

Psychological research has long-since established that, despite the best of intentions, the personal beliefs and expectations of scientists sometimes influence their research results. Indeed, some investigators have gone so far as to refer to science as "a history of corrected mistakes."[8] This sort of bias is all the more likely when it comes to the study of supernatural phenomena, which tend to be investigated — when they are investigated at all — by groups and individuals with a strong vested interest in finding for or against them.

People of faith can legitimately be suspected of a bias in favor of miracles, and this may undermine their best efforts at objectivity. But those Shroud scientists whose analysis turned up paint pigment where it didn't exist evidently fell prey to the same tendency to find what they confidently expected to find. People who make their livings or professional reputations "debunking" claims of the supernatural are not immune to the very errors of which they accuse believers.

Of course, this is not to deny that determined skeptics provide a much-needed balance. The world is full of overly credulous individuals who are much too quick to assign supernatural origins to events whose causes are not readily apparent. For example, James Randi, aka "The Amazing Randi," is a popular stage illusionist who has done a great deal to demystify apparently miraculous phenomena by showing how trickery can be used to mislead the unwary. Some years ago, for example, he exposed Reverend Peter Popoff, a prominent faith healer whose apparent omniscience about the personal affairs of members of his audience was made possible by a confederate backstage. As it turned out, she read the congregation's prayer requests, and then communicated the information they contained to Popov through a microphone hidden in his ear.

In his book *Flim-Flam! Psychics, ESP, Unicorns and Other Delusions*, Randi explains many ways in which miracles have been simulated.[9] For instance, one common ploy used by faith healers is to have their assistants offer to place older people who walk with difficulty in wheelchairs when they enter the tent or auditorium. The solicitous confederate then wheels the individual to an area near the stage. Later, when the revivalist "heals" them and they rise and walk, it creates a very impressive spectacle for those who are unaware that these people could have come in under their own power.

While there is no question that unscrupulous people throughout history have faked miracles in order to gain power and enrich themselves, we must remember that just because something *could* be simulated by trickery doesn't mean that it was actually done that way. In their enthusiasm for exposing fakery, some "debunkers" present a picture unfairly slanted in the opposite direction. In the real world, scientific research on miracles resembles the contest between a prosecutor and a defense attorney more than the conventional image of dispassionate researchers in pristine white lab coats seeking only the truth. As in a court of law, it's always a good idea to be aware of the bias of the person presenting evidence.

But the question remains: How do we go about studying an invisible supernatural force? Although God is not the sort of thing that can be seen or directly measured, neither is gravity. And just as gravity can be known by its effects on physical things, so, perhaps, can miracles. Consider, for example, George's hypothetical experiment.

GEORGE: MEASURING GOD'S HANDIWORK

When I was working on my doctorate in experimental psychology, one of the class requirements was to design a study that would prove or disprove the existence of God. The professor's purpose in giving the assignment was, obviously, to show us all that there was no conceivable way to do this. However, I still have fond memories of an ingenious research design proposed by one of my classmates.

George began his proposal with a literature review citing a passage from the Old Testament to the effect that if any man cursed God, God would instantly strike him down. Proceeding on the assumptions that God had inspired this biblical statement and that God would not lie, my friend went on to design the following experiment to test the hypothesis that God existed.

It involved hiring undergraduate volunteers to go out into a field and form three groups: one would curse God, another would praise God, and a third group of control subjects would talk among themselves. The object was, of course, to compare the rate at which subjects in the three groups were struck down by lightning, plagues, meteorites, and so forth. George planned to assess the anticipated carnage from the shade of a nearby tree, and then analyze the mortality rates of the three groups.

My friend has always maintained that had it not been for a few "bleeding hearts" on the University Human Subjects Committee, the world would by now know for sure whether God exists. George concedes that a few undergraduates might have lost their lives, but as he so philosophically observes, "What kind of a life does an undergraduate have, anyway?"

Strangely enough, I now think that in some respects George was on the right track. While we cannot test for the existence of a supernatural power directly, we may be able to do so indirectly if God intervenes in human affairs in any sort of predictable manner. After all, if the Deity really went in for divine retribution of the sort George's experiment assumed, his proposed study just might have worked (although in that case one wonders if that shade tree would have afforded him all the protection he might have needed).

We may not be able to see the "hand of God" directly, but perhaps we can identify God's handiwork in the form of surprising positive reversals of fortune that occur with unexpected frequency when certain specifiable conditions are met. We would be observing the conditions under which God, or one of God's agents, is supposed to intervene and seeing that miraculous effects do, in fact, appear.

Personal Experimentation

The vast majority of the world's inhabitants believe in the supernatural. It is my belief that many of them do so not out of ignorant superstition but because profound personal experiences have convinced them that they have a relationship with some sort of omniscient supreme Being that cares what happens to them.

Each time an individual in need returns his or her mind to peace, follows inner guidance, and pays attention to what happens next, it constitutes a small, private experiment on the reality of divine intervention. Furthermore, by continually putting their beliefs to this sort of empirical test, some spiritually oriented people are actually behaving more scientifically than those who refuse to even consider the evidence for miracles.

Scientists are not at liberty to simply define God out of existence, as naturalists once attempted to do. This is reminiscent of the logic used by the French Academy of Sciences in the eighteenth century, when that august body declared that all reports of meteorites must be fraudulent, since it was self-evidently absurd to think that rocks could fall out of the sky. It's high time that we stop pontificating about what can exist and humbly take stock of reality to find out what *does* exist.

Things to Think About

1) Scientific evidence is of limited impact when it comes to our deepest convictions, and this is as it should be.

2) Do you experience yourself as a complex robot behaving as you have been programmed to, or as a thinking, caring being who is responsible for the choices you make?

3) We may not be able to see God, but we might be able to see evidence that God intervenes to protect people who think and behave in certain specifiable ways.

Chapter Four

Deflecting Attacks

When a brother behaves insanely you can heal him only by
perceiving the sanity in him.

— *A Course in Miracles*

This chapter examines situations where a frightening,
seemingly life-threatening assault turns out harmlessly,
but these incidents inevitably raise the question about whether
the danger was real to begin with. The person telling the
story may feel that his or her actions or reactions changed
the course of the attack, but it's reasonable to wonder
whether anything *would* have happened. Maybe these folks
simply misread the cues. Perhaps their assailants never seriously intended to hurt them; perhaps the attackers created a
sense of "danger" to instill fear and cooperation but never
meant to follow through on their threats of harm. How can

we conclude that a miraculous rescue occurred when we have only the victim's opinion about what happened?

These are reasonable questions that may be impossible to answer objectively, but that's no reason to dismiss a person's subjective reality. The people who shared these accounts all had good reasons to believe that someone meant serious harm to them. Yet in spite of this conviction, they responded to their situation with peace, compassion, and even humor. Imagine how you would feel and act if the same thing were happening to you. Does the person's response seem ordinary and natural in the circumstances, or is it surprising? If someone put a knife to your throat and abducted you, would you expect to feel relaxed and loving, or terrified and filled with rage?

ELIZABETH: BALLERINAS 1, COMMANDOS 0

On her way back to her car after a ballet class in Hollywood, Elizabeth remembers passing a tall, rough-looking man who sought eye contact with her. An experienced city dweller, she quickly averted her gaze and hurried on.

Upon reaching her vehicle in a dark, deserted lot, Elizabeth warily paused a moment to make sure no one was hiding in or around it. Reassured, she unlocked the door, and that was when she was silently seized from behind. Her assailant forced an expert hand under her tongue to keep her from screaming. He shoved her into the car and followed her inside, brandishing a knife. Despite the dim light, Elizabeth had no trouble recognizing the man she had seen a few moments earlier on the street.

Although she was terrified, Elizabeth says that she felt

oddly comforted by the fact that the weapon the man was holding at her throat was only a serrated steak knife. Not that it wouldn't have done the trick, she knew, but somehow it suggested to her that her attacker was not an experienced criminal. Someone who had done this many times, she thought, would have had a different kind of weapon.

"Just calm down and keep quiet," the man ordered, seizing her keys and starting the car. "I'm not going to hurt you."

"Well, that's pretty hard to believe with that knife in my face," Elizabeth gasped. "You'd better get out of my car. I've got to get home. My little boy is waiting for me. He'll be worried to death." Ignoring her protests, the man drove off, although he repeated his assurance that he was not going to hurt her.

Somehow her mention of her son started him talking. The man seemed to *need* to talk. He said he had been a commando in Vietnam and that he had seen many children weeping over the bodies of their dead mothers. Elizabeth sensed that the idea of those motherless children still got to him, so she continued to emphasize that she was a single parent with a helpless child waiting at home. Perhaps he would hesitate to be responsible for another grieving orphan.

The man drove them to his own car and ordered her to get into it. Elizabeth balked.

"What are you going to do to me?" she demanded apprehensively.

"Why does every white woman think a black man wants to fuck her?" the kidnapper snapped bitterly. "I told you I wasn't going to hurt you. Just shut up and get into the car! I'll have you back here in twenty minutes."

Elizabeth did as she was told, and her assailant drove into the Watts ghetto of Los Angeles. He finally pulled to the curb in a semideserted business district. By now it was about ten or eleven at night. A few incurious pedestrians hurried by on the sidewalk, but Elizabeth knew better than to anticipate any help from that quarter. Suddenly, her kidnapper reached over and stuck his hands down her pants. Apparently he was planning to molest her right there in the car.

"Well, isn't this just great!" Elizabeth snapped indignantly. "You tell me you aren't going to rape me, and then the first thing you do is make a grab for me! This is exactly what you said you weren't going to do! I can see now that you are not a man of your word! How am I supposed to believe anything you say when you lie to me this way?"

Her assailant froze, stunned by her angry outburst. But Elizabeth had plenty more to say. "I suppose it was all a lie that you weren't going to hurt me, too!" she continued contemptuously. "You should be ashamed of yourself, a big man like you, taking advantage of a woman! And not only that, but lying to me after I trusted you! And besides, what time is it?"

Her captor appeared confused by her assertive behavior and the question she had fired at him. "Why? What do you mean?"

"You said you'd have me back to my car in twenty minutes. That's what you promised. But is that what you're doing? No! It's more than twenty minutes already, and here you are behaving this way! You should be ashamed of yourself, treating a woman like this!"

Her captor seemed taken aback by the authority with

which she berated him. Her manner was that of a parent who is not about to tolerate any "funny business" from a wayward child. Despite the similarity of their ages, her indignant tone said, "If you think for a minute that I'm going to put up with this, young man, you'd better think again!"

Elizabeth said that she was surprised to find that she was now absolutely fearless and self-confident to the point of truculence. The shock and terror she had felt earlier were magically gone. As far as she was concerned, she was completely in charge. I asked Elizabeth what she had imagined herself to be doing.

"I think I was trying to get through to his higher self," she replied. "I sensed that this was basically a decent guy who had taken a wrong turn that night, out of some personal desperation. He'd been trained as a killer in Vietnam and had probably seen and done some pretty revolting things. My guess is that civilian life wasn't working out very well, and he was wondering why he shouldn't just take whatever he wanted by force.

"In a way, I guess you could say I was telling him 'why not.' Because it was dishonorable. Because it hurt innocent people. Because it made children suffer. My intuitive sense of him was that he was in a lot of conflict about taking advantage of a woman this way. I think that he was a man who normally took pride in living up to his word."

Whatever fantasy this veteran had had of how the assault would go, it apparently didn't involve a woman looking him in the eye and indignantly reminding him of his responsibilities as a man. Elizabeth's speech took the wind out of his sails. Her assailant yanked away from her with a baffled and aggrieved look and sat staring at her in perplexity. He seemed uncertain how to proceed.

"How much money do you have?" he finally demanded.

"I don't have much," Elizabeth replied. "About fifteen dollars. How about if I give you half?"

The man shook his head, stunned. "Jesus Christ! I don't believe you!" he burst out, pounding the steering wheel in frustration. This was not the way abducted women were supposed to behave.

"Well, you can't blame me for trying," replied Elizabeth coolly. "This is all the money I have. I've got a three-year-old son to support, you know. You're not the only one who has problems."

"Give me the money!" the man ordered angrily. He seemed utterly flummoxed, and it struck Elizabeth that he was backing down from whatever he had planned to do to her and was settling for the cash. She handed it over without further comment, and he quickly started the engine and wrenched the vehicle back into traffic. On the way back to her car, he held the knife against her ribs and said menacingly, "If you make a sound, you'll be sorry!"

"I won't make a sound," Elizabeth agreed meekly.

"He had to act like he was in charge," she told me, "but at that point, I think we both knew that it was over. He was just saving face. He couldn't bring himself to hurt me."

Pulling up a block or so from her car, the man angrily shouted, "Get out of here!" But before she could open the door, he added in impotent fury, "Look at me! *You* did this to me!"

Elizabeth looked over and saw that his face was a mask

of anguish and that it was streaming with perspiration. He was obviously in a state of powerful emotional turmoil, and his distress touched her heart. Turning back to him, she reached over and tenderly cradled his face in her hands. Looking deep into his eyes, she found herself quietly saying, "The next time you feel this way, I hope you'll realize that what you really need is to reach out and touch someone. This is about communication. There are a lot of ways to make contact with people, and I hope that next time you'll pick a different one from the one you chose tonight. You don't need to act this way. You're a good man. This isn't who you are."

As Elizabeth gazed into the man's eyes, she suddenly felt his defenses fall away. He seemed to open to her and become vulnerable. It was a moment of incredible intimacy. A current of pure love passed between them that was so intoxicating that Elizabeth says it made her feel as if she was high on a drug.

So caught up was she in the compassion she felt for her would-be assailant that she experienced an overwhelming desire to help him. "You're not going to believe this," she told me ruefully, "but I actually had to restrain myself from giving him my phone number so that he could call me if he ever needed someone to talk to! I realized that that would be absolutely insane, and I didn't actually do it. But in that moment I loved him so much. I just wanted to show him that someone cared about him and that he didn't have to try to get affection from people by force." Suppressing the impulse, she got out of his car and hurried to her own.

Elizabeth was still in an exalted state as she drove to her house. She said that it was as if she had undergone a "spiritual revelation." She felt giddy and invincible. When she finally arrived home much later than expected, her boyfriend, who had been babysitting her son, met her at the door with evident concern.

"Where on earth have you *been?*" he demanded anxiously.

At these words, Elizabeth felt herself crumble. Although she had been supremely self-confident during and after the incident itself, she suddenly fell back into ordinary consciousness and quite literally went into shock. She began to shake uncontrollably. Her teeth chattered, and her friend had to wrap her in a blanket and hold her tight for a long time before she could pull herself together enough to tell him what had happened. Now that it was over, she could scarcely believe the masterful way she had handled herself only a short time before.

Today, Elizabeth remembers her assailant with affection. "I still think about that guy all the time and wonder what happened to him. I hope he's okay. I was really lucky. What I did wouldn't have worked with everyone. He was really a good man. I like to think that he was as deeply affected by our encounter as I was and that he never did anything like that again."

Like Ashley in chapter 1, Elizabeth seemed to lock onto an image of her assailant as a good man and then insist that he live up to it. When he attempted to assault her sexually, she reminded him that this was not an appropriate way for a decent person like him to behave. Was he, or was he not, an honorable man?

Indeed, I am left with the impression that, with the help of divine guidance, Elizabeth overcame her assailant in some sort of contest of wills. He had the knife, the strong physique, and the commando training, yet by the end of their encounter he was a broken man, rebuking Elizabeth for what *she* had done to *him*. There is something both pathetic and ludicrous about his final accusation. How does an unarmed ballerina make a highly trained, knife-wielding commando beg for mercy?

The dynamics of miraculous deliverance become even clearer in the case of Kathleen, below. Like Elizabeth, some of the people who told me their stories seemed to slip imperceptibly over the border between terror and the "peace that passeth understanding." Others, like Kathleen, had to struggle mightily to keep fear at bay. Unlike most of the people who told me of their narrow escapes, Kathleen was aware of the creative power of consciousness. She understood exactly what she would have to do to save her life, and her only uncertainty seemed to be about her ability to do it.

KATHLEEN: STOP IN THE NAME OF LOVE

At age twenty-three, Kathleen was returning home from a waitress job at 2 A.M. when she realized that a car was following hers. It was still there after stops at a gas station and an all-night market, so Kathleen took evasive action, making a series of sudden turns through the deserted San Francisco streets. Thinking she had lost the tail, she drove on to her apartment.

When she got out of her car, however, Kathleen saw that

the man who'd been following her had caught up. He intercepted her on foot as she crossed the street, but Kathleen remembers that even then she was not particularly worried. She was right outside her house, and he was a rather small man. She was used to dealing with guys who couldn't take a hint and did not anticipate that this was going to be a particularly difficult situation. The man attempted to start a conversation, but Kathleen brushed him off in a friendly way and started to walk on by. At that point, he pulled a gun out of his pocket.

Kathleen said that when she saw the gun, she instantly burst into tears. "All I can tell you is that at that moment, I realized that all of the rules of the universe had changed — that nothing was the way I had thought it was, or ever would be again. I can't tell you how completely disorienting it is to realize that something like this could happen to *you!*"

The gunman ordered her to get back into her car, and he drove to a nearby park. All the way there, Kathleen felt as though she were in shock. She wondered numbly if she should try to jump out of the moving vehicle, but he had the gun trained on her the whole way, and she couldn't see that she could get far on the deserted streets even if she was not badly injured in the fall.

When they reached the park, it clicked into place that the police had been finding women's bodies there almost weekly. It had been the talk of the neighborhood for a long time now. Her assailant ordered her out of the car and into the woods. Kathleen offered him the money in her purse, but he was not interested.

Instead, he told her that he was going to rape and murder her. He said that he regretted having to kill her — he never enjoyed doing it — but that there was just no other way now that she had seen his face.

It was then that Kathleen found herself going into an unusual state of consciousness. Her senses felt heightened, and the smells and sounds of the woods were deeply etched in her mind. At the same time, she was completely unaware of the cold. She said that there was a strange lightness about her, and that she suddenly went from revulsion and fear to feeling completely peaceful and loving toward her captor.

"It's hard to explain, and I feel really embarrassed about it now. I felt detached about what was going on. It just seemed like it was going to be all right. At the same time, I felt like I loved this guy. It was so bizarre! I went into a peculiar state of mind where I was just like an angel in my body, radiating love and compassion to this man who was planning to kill me!"

Her assailant ordered her to walk through some heavy underbrush and continued to wave the gun around and talk graphically about the things he was going to do to her. Every time he mentioned killing her, Kathleen mentally brushed it aside, resolutely thinking instead, "No, you won't do that."

In retrospect, Kathleen said that she felt that her previous experimentation with psychedelic drugs had given her an inner experience of the way reality is created by the thoughts held in consciousness. It was very clear to her that she must not become fearful or in any way entertain the possibility that the man would kill her.

Kathleen emphasized that her refusal to do so was based upon her own choice, not on her reading of the man she was with. It was clear to her that he had murdered other women and seriously intended to do the same to her. Nevertheless, she invested totally in the conviction that he could not possibly kill her. She said that she structured her personal reality in such a way as to cast him as a person who would see that she was someone who deserved kindness.

As they blundered through the undergrowth in the dark, Kathleen began to talk to her assailant in a casual, friendly way. She said that it was hard for her to walk and asked if it would be all right to take his arm. He agreed, and she clung to him for support, aware that she was creating in every way possible the atmosphere of two people on a date.

Years later, Kathleen laughed in embarrassment and perplexity as she told this part. "I kept acting dependent and trying to get him to take care of me. Like I was a lady in distress and he was a kind gentleman I was relying upon for help. It was as though I was trying to get him to play Rhett Butler to my Scarlet O'Hara!"

When they came to a clearing, Kathleen kept talking in a relaxed, chatty manner from the peaceful altered state she had fallen into. Like Ashley Smith, she talked about herself, trying to help her assailant recognize her as a real person with feelings like his own, and she asked him questions about himself, some of which he answered. They sat together on the ground for a long time just talking, as Kathleen radiated angelic compassion to this man who was about to rape and murder her.

When he waved the gun around, Kathleen confided that just seeing it made her afraid, and she asked if he would mind very much just putting it out of sight so she would not have to look at it. He did so. Kathleen said that he pulled it out a number of times, obviously getting off on the macho display, but each time she very sweetly asked him to put it away and he did. Her feminine dependence upon his kindness probably gave him an alternative way to feel powerful by being gallant instead of by hurting her.

Finally, he did rape her. With a gun to her head, Kathleen did not resist. Although it was an awful experience, she remained in the peaceful, loving altered state throughout, and she treated him with kindness and compassion despite what was happening. "I actually apologized to him for the fact that my body wasn't producing any lubrication. Did you ever hear anything so sick?! I have always been so ashamed of myself for acting that way, but at the time I was only concerned with being kind to him."

Kathleen emphasizes that, as strange as it sounds even to her, her behavior was not an act. She really felt detached and loving and absolutely confident that there was kindness in this man that would keep him from killing her. By focusing totally upon that goodness, she felt she could bring it to the surface.

When he was through raping her, he said that he had changed his mind. Maybe he would not kill her after all. But she must never tell anyone about what had happened. Kathleen promised without hesitation and thanked him sincerely for sparing her life. They drove back to Kathleen's apartment, and he told her to sit in her car until he passed her in his. She did so, although she again had to resist the fear that he would shoot her as he drove by. However, he went on his way without further incident.

Kathleen reported the rape to the police immediately, but they were unable to find her assailant. Soon afterward she bought a gun and carried it with her for several years. Despite her peaceful, loving altered state at the time, she experienced tremendous rage about the incident when it was over and is convinced that she could easily kill anyone who threatened her that way again.

She finds the disparity between her feelings during and after the incident profoundly confusing. "It was like being an angel for a little while. That's all I can tell you. I didn't feel as though I was pretending to care deeply about him — I really felt that way."

Kathleen also felt a lot of shame when the incident was over. In retrospect, she thought that she had behaved in a cowardly fashion, being so nice to someone who was putting her through such an experience. Now a marriage, family, and child counselor, Kathleen is aware of concepts like the Stockholm syndrome, named for a 1973 incident in that city where four people developed a loving alliance with the bank robbers who held them hostage for six days. Months after being freed by police, two of the female hostages actually became engaged to two of the robbers, and all of the hostages continued to have warm feelings for these men.

Without attempting to analyze the psychodynamics of the hostages in Stockholm, I believe that what Kathleen and Elizabeth felt for their attackers was an impersonal spiritual love that compassionately embraces all beings. I think they, and indeed all of the people who shared their assault stories with me, actually moved to a level of consciousness where nothing was real for them except love. This will be discussed in greater detail in chapter 12, which focuses on ego dynamics.

Certainly Kathleen was very clear about the life-or-death

importance of remaining in that fearless, loving state of consciousness. "Every time he threatened me, I knew he meant it, and I had to work to keep the fear from coming in. I was very aware of using the power of my mind to make the situation turn out okay. Not that rape is okay, but it's a lot better than murder!

"I knew that if I let the possibility of his killing me into my mind, it could manifest in physical reality and that I had just better not do that! Every time he threatened me, I would think, 'Oh, no. That isn't really what's going to happen. You think you mean it, but you wouldn't really do that to me.' I know how nutty this sounds, but the fact is I feel sure even now that if I had allowed the possibility of his murdering me to exist in my reality, it would have happened."

Kathleen's assailant was a self-confessed serial murderer as well as a rapist, and there is little reason to doubt that he was ready to carry out his threat to kill her. Somehow, by becoming "an angel in my body," she persuaded him to spare her life. In the next story, Debra tells a remarkably similar tale of meeting a mortal threat with love.

Debra: The Disarming Power of Love

Debra entered her Beverly Hills home one afternoon to be confronted by two masked men with automatic weapons. She turned and ran for the door but was roughly tackled from behind, dragged into the bedroom, and tied hand and foot on the bed. The men, speaking with heavy Middle Eastern accents, demanded that Debra open the safe for them, but she explained that she did not know the combination. They taped a mask over her face so that she could neither see nor speak and told her that they would wait for Debra's husband to come home, force him to open the safe with the threat that they would kill her otherwise, and then murder them both.

These Arab terrorists said that they had picked Debra's house because she and her husband were wealthy Jews. Throughout the afternoon, while one of the men ransacked her home, the other held an automatic rifle to Debra's head. Despite the conviction that death was imminent, Debra was surprised to find that she was not afraid.

"It was as though I was out of my body, and I know I must have been in some sort of altered state," she told me. "You know how when you have your nails done you can't go to the bathroom for a while because it would mess them up? Well, I was just returning from a manicure when I came home that day. I was racing for the bathroom — maybe if I hadn't been in such a hurry, I would have noticed that something was wrong sooner.

"Anyway, they threw me on the bed on my stomach and tied my hands to my feet behind my back. I know I was in an altered state because it was three hours later before I got free, but I don't remember the slightest discomfort, either from the ropes or my bladder."

Debra found her mind poised in a place of perfect inner peace. Despite the tape over her mouth, she eventually worked open a small gap through which she could talk, and she began to converse with the man holding her at gunpoint. Debra is a friendly, outgoing person, but it was bizarre hearing her account of a very ordinary chat in such extraordinary circumstances.

Debra got her assailant, a displaced Palestinian, talking

about his home in Lebanon and his family. As the afternoon wore on, he spoke to her very openly about missing his son, about jobs he had held in the United States, and about terrorist activities he had taken part in, including the murder of witnesses like herself. He detailed his grievances against the Jews, and Debra found herself deeply moved by the suffering he and his people had experienced.

In her altered state, Debra felt a compassion for this man and his partner, which she finds hard to explain. They seemed to her to be precious souls, and her heart ached for the pain that had driven them to lives of violence. She found herself encouraging and comforting the one who held the gun to her head, and she was unaware of any fear, although she did not doubt that he would kill her.

In the course of the long afternoon, the other terrorist finished searching the house and decided to rape Debra. However, his partner, with whom she had developed a relationship, would not permit it. The two men argued heatedly for a long time.

After three hours, Debra's husband arrived. The men forced him to open the safe and then tied him up on the bed next to her.

"Do you love your wife?" the man with whom she had been speaking unexpectedly demanded of her husband.

"Yes," he replied.

"Tell her so now!" the terrorist ordered.

As her husband said, "I love you, Debra," both of them were convinced that these would be the last words they would ever hear on earth. But then the men silently stole away. They moved so quietly that neither she nor her husband heard them go, but Debra said that she could *feel* them withdraw, as though she were lovingly connected to them in some way.

When the two finally got free and called the police, the authorities were astonished that Debra had not been raped and that both had not been murdered. The police readily identified their assailants as the ones who had committed other, similar crimes, and they had never before left a witness alive. Further, it seemed strange that they would have confided personal information to Debra unless they fully expected that she would not live to repeat it.

Since she had not seen her attackers' faces, Debra could see little point in looking at mug shots. However, the police were pretty sure they knew who the men were from the style of the attack and were anxious for her to try to identify them on the chance that she had seen them in the neighborhood casing the house beforehand.

When eventually prevailed upon to go through the books of photographs, Debra confidently picked out the pictures of both men the police had in mind from among hundreds of others. She was astonished by the self-assurance of her choices, despite having no recollection of ever having seen their faces before. While she cannot discount the police hypothesis that she may have seen them in the neighborhood, she is personally convinced that she did not. Instead, she feels that she somehow recognized their inner being from intimate acquaintance.

Debra says that she was so focused on the goodness that she saw in these men just below the surface that she felt nothing for them but unconditional love. It seemed to her as though she left her body and some loving presence took over for her. Even now when she tells the story, she feels as though it happened to someone else. It is difficult for her to refer to the men as "terrorists" because the term sounds so violent, and she experienced them as precious and gentle. She has long felt that she will never adequately explain that state to anyone else.

Is it possible that by overlooking her assailants' hostility — or as Ashley Smith put it, not judging them — and focusing totally upon their basic goodness, Debra brought that goodness into manifestation? The more stories like this I hear, the more difficult it becomes to dismiss the idea that a peaceful, loving state of consciousness is instrumental in turning away violence. Clearly, the people in jeopardy in these stories believe that it was. Or is it only a coincidence that an unconditionally loving mental state keeps cropping up in the experience of people who escape death at the last minute? More importantly, how many times must two events *coincide* before we begin to seriously consider the possibility that a causal relationship — rather than chance — connects them?

Things to Think About

1) Miracles seem to occur when we decide to come from love despite the fact that the situation appears to call for terror or rage.

2) You can hate or fear an assailant, or have a miracle heal the situation, but you can't do both.

Chapter Five

Fat Chance!

Chance is perhaps the pseudonym of God
when he does not wish to sign.

— *Anatole France*

W hen a person mistakenly attributes an event to a supernatural cause — for example, imagining that a bad
thing happened because someone walked under a ladder or
broke a mirror — we properly call it *superstition*. But to suggest that all attributions of events to supernatural causes can
be reduced to superstition is, in my opinion, going too far.
When, after extensive searching, no adequate physical cause
can be found for a particular turn of events, it is reasonable to
at least consider the possibility of causes beyond the physical.

The way committed naturalists respond to apparently
inexplicable occurrences is to simply assume that they must
have had a physical cause that has not yet been discovered.

While this is often the case, the assumption effectively precludes consideration of alternative, miraculous explanations. This logic reminds me of the old joke about the inebriate who is searching for his lost keys under a streetlight. When a helpful passerby asks him where, precisely, he lost his keys, the man replies, "Back there in the alley. But the light's better out here."

Just as the keys will never be found within the conveniently illuminated area being searched, I'm convinced that the true and complete explanations for some phenomena are not to be found within the physical world. Naturalists sometimes rationalize their inability to discover adequate causal relationships within the circumscribed area they are prepared to examine by resorting to the all-purpose explanation that the event must simply have been due to chance. This is to say that we must simply take it on faith that random factors can account for every inexplicable thing that occurs in our world.

An example of this reasoning is the old saw that if a troop of monkeys was locked in a room for all eternity with a typewriter and enough paper, it would eventually produce all of the world's great novels. Indeed, the naturalist philosophy holds that even the most highly skillful expressions of human intelligence and creativity are actually the result of unthinking evolutionary processes.

But, despite the fact that we may sometimes pay lip service to this view, we aren't so foolish as to actually behave as though we really believe it. The fact is that while an enormous number of things are theoretically *possible*, most are so *improbable* that we cannot really bring ourselves to believe they have actually occurred. The same person who insists that in theory a monkey could write *Pride and Prejudice* will laugh at you if you try to prove that a monkey actually *did* type an intelligible sentence.

Why do we feel so free to dismiss chance as the true explanation for certain highly improbable events? As the distinguished physical chemist and philosopher of science Michael Polanyi explains:

> A probability statement cannot be strictly contradicted by any event, however improbable this event may appear in its light. The contradiction must be established by a personal act of appraisal which rejects certain possibilities as being too improbable to be entertained as true.[1]

Perhaps the most familiar example of an arena where such "personal acts of appraisal" are explicitly acknowledged as the basis for decision making is a court of law. There, the jury must decide whether various words and deeds of the defendant indicate guilt, or whether their apparent consistency with criminal intent was purely coincidental. As an example, let's look at the Scott Peterson murder trial.

Scott Peterson: Convicted Without a Witness

When Scott Peterson's pregnant wife, Laci, disappeared on Christmas Eve 2002 in the San Francisco Bay Area, Peterson represented himself as a loving husband who wanted nothing more than to find her alive and well. But as police investigated, an enormous amount of circumstantial evidence built up against him, and Peterson was eventually accused of murder. This evidence included his affair with another woman, the fact that he told his lover that he had "lost" his wife weeks before she actually disappeared, and the fact that on the day his wife vanished he had been fishing in the same marina where her body, and the body of their unborn son, were later found.

In addition, traces of cement were detected on Peterson's boat, and when he thought he wasn't being watched, Peterson repeatedly returned to the marina to stand and stare at the water and the shore near the place where the bodies were eventually recovered. He'd also recently taken out a $250,000 insurance policy on Laci, and over time, numerous lies he told police and the public came to light.

But there were no actual witnesses who saw him commit murder, and the prosecution was unable to come up with a single piece of definitive, direct evidence, such as the murder weapon, linking Peterson with the deaths of his wife and unborn child.

Just because a man has an affair doesn't necessarily mean he wants to kill his wife. Many would lie to seduce a woman, cover up an affair, or make themselves look better, and lots of innocent people take out new insurance policies when they are expecting a child. Even the fact that he was fishing the day she disappeared in the marina where the bodies were subsequently found doesn't mean he was the murderer. Perhaps that really was just a strange coincidence. Or perhaps the real killer planted the bodies there to incriminate Peterson.

Nevertheless, despite the fact that each individual piece of evidence was open to a variety of interpretations, the jury convicted Peterson of the crime. The fact is that when too many odd coincidences all point in the same direction, common sense kicks in to tell us that if it looks like a duck, walks like a duck, and quacks like a duck, there's a really good chance it's a duck. Even with the stakes as high as a human life (Peterson was potentially subject to the death penalty for this crime), we understand that there is a difference between "a possible doubt" and "a reasonable doubt."

Using Our Common Sense

Michael Polanyi offers an example that makes this point even more concrete.[2] Imagine that we look out of a train window and observe that there are rocks on a nearby hillside arranged in such a way as to spell out the phrase: "Welcome to Bridgeport." *Bridgeport* happens to be the name of the town through which we are passing.

We instantly assume that the rocks were placed there intentionally by humans. We know that it is *theoretically possible* for rocks to roll down a hillside and accidentally arrange themselves in a seemingly meaningful way — and in this case, not just *any* meaningful way, but into English words spelling a geographically appropriate greeting. However, we also recognize that it is *astronomically improbable* that this is the true explanation for the phenomenon.

We might readily accept the idea that falling rocks had accidentally formed a single letter, but not the precise sequence of letters that just happens to spell out a greeting involving the correct name of the railway stop. While coincidence is undeniably a *possible* explanation, there is a far simpler one available that experience tells us is also infinitely more likely to be true — that the rocks were placed as they were by someone who wanted to welcome travelers and inform them about their present location.

If a traveling companion remarked upon the "incredible coincidence" of the rocks accidentally spelling out this greeting, we'd assume that he or she was joking. Indeed, we'd expect any child old enough to read the message to realize that it *could not* be the product of coincidence. The meaningfulness of the result constitutes convincing evidence that it was created intentionally with some intelligible purpose in mind.

MEANINGFUL VERSUS MEANINGLESS COINCIDENCES

Coincidence properly refers to a constellation of events, two or more of which accidentally share some common feature. The common element gives coincidences an intriguing, superficial resemblance to meaningful, intentionally organized events. They look as though they might mean something, but — being only random occurrences — they don't.

For instance, if I am on my way to a particular store in my car just when a commercial for that store plays on my radio, I might deem it a mere coincidence. Two events which have something in common, and both of which are fairly rare, happened to coincide quite by accident. What does it mean that I happened to hear the commercial while on the way to the store? Probably nothing. That is why we tend to call such coincidences "mere."

But when coincidences are *too* appropriate to the needs of those involved, we tend to abandon the idea that they *are* coincidences, and we suspect instead that some hidden intention is directing the outcome. For instance, a woman I know named Alana once told me that when she was a starving student, she became very ill with a serious throat infection. The doctor at the student health clinic wrote her a prescription for antibiotics, but she discovered that filling it would cost three dollars. She didn't even have one dollar, so she started wearily home without the medicine. However, something caught her eye in the snow beside the walkway as she left the clinic. When she investigated, she found three crisp dollar bills.

To hear three dollars mentioned and then encounter three dollars in the snow might be a mere coincidence. But for Alana to "accidentally" find three dollars just when she so badly needed exactly that amount qualifies as what psychiatrist Carl Jung[3] called a "synchronous experience" — one where there is a strange and deeply meaningful correspondence between an internal event (Alana's perceived need for three dollars) and an external event (the unexpected discovery of precisely that amount beside the clinic walkway). Here, circumstances appear to be arranging themselves with an intelligible purpose in mind. Indeed, events in the physical world are behaving the way we ourselves might behave if we wanted to help Alana.

Or, consider the following example of a synchronous experience involving the famous actor Anthony Hopkins.[4] I once read that when Hopkins won a leading role in *The Girl from Petrovka*, he was eager to read the novel from which the screenplay had come, but he was unable to find a copy in London. One day when he was passing through Leicester Square, he noticed a discarded book lying on a bench and was curious enough to pick it up. It was *The Girl from Petrovka*.

Later, during filming, Hopkins met the author, George Feifer, and mentioned how hard it had been to find his novel. Feifer agreed and told him that he no longer had a copy of the book himself, having loaned his last one to a friend who had lost it in London. Hopkins graciously gave him the book he'd found on the bench, and when Feifer opened it, he saw that it was annotated in his own handwriting. The book Hopkins had given him was the very same volume Feifer's friend had lost! (Cue theme from *The Twilight Zone*.)

Harvey: The Shock of a Lifetime

Or consider this story. I was once chatting with a faculty colleague named Harvey over lunch in his office. We were talking of this and that when the concept of synchronicity came up, and Harvey expressed complete skepticism. We debated the point with much good-humored kidding back and forth.

Harvey eventually remarked that he hadn't enjoyed a good argument about synchronicity in years. In fact, the last time was with a young woman who had been a friend of his daughter's. Her name was Penny, and as Harvey traveled back in memory he got a faraway look.

"You know, I don't think I've thought about Penny in the last fifteen years. It's funny how people can be so important in your life at one point and then just pass out of it without a trace. I wonder whatever happened to her?"

My friend and I went back to our discussion of synchronicity, but it was soon interrupted by a phone call. Harvey froze as he listened to the voice on the other end. He stammered a reply and then covered the mouthpiece with his hand and croaked, "It's Penny!"

When the call was over, Harvey looked dazed. He reported that Penny had said she just happened to be thinking about the old days and had an urge to see if he was still at the same number.

"I suppose you're going to say this is evidence for synchronicity," Harvey laughed nervously.

"I suppose I am," I agreed.

To me, Jung's synchronous experiences appear to represent divine intervention in less dire situations than those where miracles of deliverance are required. Alana's experience of finding the money she needed in the snow occupies the border between synchronous and deliverance experiences since it did "rescue" her from further anxiety and illness. The examples involving Anthony Hopkins and my friend Harvey, on the other hand, are more purely synchronous. They seem to me to demonstrate the fact that minds are connected, though Harvey's experience was perhaps intended to prompt him to reconsider his position on paranormal phenomena.

None of these stories can properly be called coincidental since to say that a circumstance is meaningful and fulfills an intelligible purpose is to suggest that it is not really a random event. In synchronous experiences, it is as if a larger mind that is aware of our circumstances, thoughts, and needs is arranging events in the physical world so as to supply needed resources or information. When a person or an animal arranges the physical environment so as to accomplish a desirable end, we conclude that it is acting intelligently. When the universe behaves in the same way, is it unreasonable to wonder if it, too, may be intelligent?

CRITERIA FOR DISTINGUISHING
MIRACLES FROM COINCIDENCES

But how can we tell whether a particular coincidence is "mere" or "meaningful"? Researchers in the social sciences usually try to distinguish coincidences from meaningful relationships by estimating how likely it is that the result they received *could have* occurred by chance. If the odds against its random occurrence are less than, say, five in a hundred, they tentatively conclude that it was probably not due to chance, label it "significant," and interpret it as support for the hypothesis they are testing.

However, while this strategy is feasible in the laboratory, it is seldom so in real life. How can we estimate the odds against Alana finding three dollars in the snow precisely when she needed them? What are the chances of Penny's call coming during a discussion of synchronicity, and right after Harvey was speaking about her for the first time in fifteen years? Common sense tells us that the odds against such things are humongous, but "humongous" is not a statistical term with which scientists can work in a rigorous fashion.

The fact is that some events are so rare and so extraordinarily meaningful that we cannot even begin to estimate how improbable they actually are. Naturalists will be content to assume that any concatenation of events must have had *some* probability of occurring by chance and let it go at that. However, those rocks on the hillside also have some probability of chance occurrence, and I, for one, would not be satisfied to attribute them to chance even if they had been found on the lunar surface welcoming the first astronaut to the moon!

In fact, I think that there are three criteria that can be used to distinguish supernatural events from coincidences. First, being random, true coincidences should be rare. It's all very well if an ad for the store I'm driving to plays on my car radio once in a while. If the appropriate commercial starts playing every time I drive to any store at all, I abandon the theory that it's just a coincidence and begin to suspect that someone is playing a trick on me. So, first, if the relationship between inner peace and miracles of deliverance is as predictable as it appears to be, these events cannot legitimately be written off as chance occurrences.

Second, scientists do not attribute an event to random factors if its occurrence is predicted by a theory. For example, most of us do not deem it a coincidence if our car starts when we turn the key in the ignition. This is precisely what we expected would happen, given what we understand about cars.

Similarly, the spiritual masters of widely diverse cultures claim that miracles become possible whenever someone goes into a peaceful, meditative state of consciousness and follows inner guidance. These positive reversals of fortune cannot be coincidental if they reliably occur as predicted by a widely held theory of the supernatural.

And third, when outcomes are uniquely meaningful and appropriate to the needs of the people involved, it is difficult to resist the conclusion that they were intentionally arranged by a loving consciousness not unlike our own. Miracles of deliverance and synchronous experiences represent organized, goal-directed behavior on the part of the universe itself. Common sense rebels against the idea that such perfectly timed and extraordinarily significant occurrences could be the product of blind chance.

MEL: HEEDING GOOD ADVICE

A perfect example of just such a uniquely meaningful coincidence happened to Mel, who was walking back from town one dark, moonless night to the children's camp where he was working as a counselor. The visibility along this little country road was so poor that he found it necessary to walk with one foot on the dirt shoulder and the other on the pavement, just to keep track of the turnings. He walked facing oncoming traffic so he would be sure to see the headlights of approaching vehicles in time to get out of their way.

As he strolled along thinking of nothing in particular, Mel suddenly heard a voice in his mind say, "Move to the left!" Mel was surprised but did nothing. The voice came again. "Move to the left, now!"

Mel had never heard a voice in his head before, and he didn't know what to make of this one, except that he wasn't about to be ordered around by it.

"No. Why should I?" he mentally demanded.

"Just do it!" the voice responded.

"No!" Mel said again. "This is silly."

"The problem with you is that no one can tell you anything," the voice retorted. "You always think you know better, and you never listen. You've been stubborn all your life. Are you completely incapable of accepting advice? No one is watching. You will not be embarrassed. Just move off the road!"

Mel's obstinacy had often been criticized by others, and he had to admit that this indictment was not entirely without basis. It was true that he usually preferred to follow his own counsel. But to say that he was *totally incapable* of accepting advice was going too far.

In order to show the voice how wrong it was, Mel made a comical balletic leap to his left. After all, he was alone in the dark, and there was no one there to observe his irrational behavior. At the moment his feet touched the ground, he felt a powerful blast of air accompanied by a swooshing sound on his right. A silent automobile, traveling without visible lights on the wrong side of the road, had just swept over the patch of pavement he had occupied a moment before. As Mel watched its red brake lights disappear around the next curve, he realized that had he not leaped to the left when he did, he would have been run over.

Once again, while we can readily estimate the likelihood of a person being hit by a car on a dark country road, there is no conceivable basis for establishing the probability of the voice that spoke to Mel. This was the only time in his life that Mel ever heard a voice in his head telling him to move to the left, and it was also the only time in his life that he ever needed such advice. To call this a coincidence seems absurd and does violence to what we ordinarily mean by the word.

In Mel's case, it is difficult to avoid the conclusion that some intelligent entity was aware of the impending danger and spoke to his mind to direct him through it. The source of this voice — whether it was a higher part of his own mind, God, an angel, a spirit guide, or something else — remains to be seen. But the voice was clearly responding appropriately to a need that Mel had no conscious way of knowing he had.

Liz: A Fantasy of the Future

Liz's story also involves an intuitive warning, this one word-less. Driving through the Mojave Desert late at night, Liz found herself drifting into fantasy. In her imagination she saw herself coming upon the scene of some sort of accident. A car was stopped on the shoulder at an odd angle, its doors standing open. A female figure was sprawled immobile on the ground beside it. A man in shirtsleeves frantically sig-naled Liz to stop and help.

In her fantasy, Liz pulled over onto the shoulder. The man ran up and yanked open the passenger-side door. His head appeared in the opening, and then Liz was jolted by the realization that there was a gun in his hand, pointed at her. The woman who had appeared to be unconscious was right behind him as he leaped into Liz's front seat.

This shocking turn of events startled her back to reality instantly. What a strange thing to imagine! Liz could not remember ever having had such a bizarre train of thought before.

Some fifteen minutes later, the scene she had imagined took shape before her in physical reality. There was the car, the inert woman's body, and the man in shirtsleeves silhouet-ted in her headlights, frantically waving her down. Every de-tail of the setting was just as it had been a few minutes earlier in her waking dream. Slowing her car, Liz stared at the scene in disbelief. The thing she had imagined was now ac-tually happening!

Liz is a tenderhearted person, and in a situation like this one she would ordinarily do precisely what she had done in her fantasy. This time, although it was hard for her, she swerved past the waving man without stopping.

Laughing guiltily at the memory, she said to me, "For all I know, they were perfectly nice people who really needed help. To this day, they are probably still talking about what a bitch I was for not stopping! But I just couldn't do it. It was too eerie after that fantasy I'd just had. Once I saw the whole scene starting all over again, I knew it was a warning, and there was just no way I was going to make the same mistake twice."

I GET SOME NEEDED REASSURANCE

I have my own synchronous experience to relate as well, this one in response to a direct appeal. Some years ago, I was driving alone from Los Angeles to Sedona, Arizona. As I sped through the high desert, I began to experience symptoms of severe anxiety. I felt agitated, and I had a recurring fantasy of my car skidding off the road.

Why would I suddenly be having an anxiety attack when I had never had one before? As I tried to sort things out, I realized that the altitude and the thin air had something to do with it. I associated thin air with mountains, and I remembered the experience I recounted in chapter 2 when my car had almost skidded over a cliff after a blowout on black ice. Although I had not been upset about the experience when it happened, I realized that my brain must have developed a phobic response to driving under similar conditions.

Anxiety made the drive across the desert miserable, and this was a disappointment because I usually love long car trips. I stopped for the night, and the next morning I drove into real mountains. The anxiety was still present, but it was tolerable.

I could comfort myself that it was late spring, and at least there would not be any snow or ice. I knew that I could just wear the anxiety out eventually if I didn't let it stop me.

Soon I began to notice snow on approaching vehicles, and I realized that there must be some up ahead. My anxiety intensified, but I kept going as driving conditions became worse. Before long, the road was rutted with ice and snow, and I was in a full-blown panic. I pulled to the side and consulted a map.

Before me lay a ten-mile stretch of two-lane road. At the end of it, I could connect with the freeway, which would be clear of snow. My lane, I could already see, wound along the outside edge of the mountain with a cliff dropping away only a few feet from the pavement. There were no safety guards to catch a skidding vehicle, and the twisting road was completely choked with snow and ice. My worst fears were realized.

I sat there staring at the map for probably ten minutes. Maybe I should just turn around and go back? It would take most of the day to retrace my path and come around the long way, but that would be better than facing that ten-mile stretch to the freeway.

In the end, I decided that I just had to go on. I love the mountains, and I knew that if I ran away now, the fear would only be worse the next time I tried driving in them. I was not prepared to give up the mountains for the rest of my life out of fear.

I started off slowly, clutching the wheel convulsively, panting with anxiety. The fantasy of sliding over the edge just a few feet away intensified like a nightmare in a horror movie. It was the most terrifying experience I have ever had.

Personally, I'm convinced that everyone has an inner guide — an awakened being who is able to communicate with our minds, as I believe Mel's guide communicated with him on that dark country road. So I made up my mind to ask my companion spirit for help in getting through the next ten miles.

I think of my guide as Jesus, so I began repeating his name over and over. If only I could feel his presence and know that he was with me, I could relax a little and get through this somehow. However, after repeating "Jesus Christ, Jesus Christ" over and over for several minutes, I had to admit that it was doing no good at all. My panic was increasing, as if that were possible!

"Okay," I told myself, "Let's think about this logically. If I am calling on Jesus, then he must be with me. It can't be that he could be unaware of my situation or ignoring it. So he must be here. But that's not helping because I can't feel his presence. I can't prevent the panic until I feel his presence, but the panic is preventing me from being aware of his presence. What the hell do I do now?"

About then, I began to have an idea that Jesus had a message for me on the radio. Now I generally consider hospitalizing my clients when they start having thoughts like this, so I quickly brushed it aside. However, it kept coming back. "Turn on the radio. I have a message for you."

"That's ridiculous," I thought. "I must really be desperate if I'm coming up with stuff like this!" Besides, I had turned off the radio forty-five minutes earlier because it was impossible to get a station in the mountains. And turning it back on would require me to remove a hand from the wheel just when it seemed as though only unceasing vigilance could get me through this alive.

But the idea wouldn't go away, and eventually I realized I'd have to turn on the radio just to get rid of it. It was distracting me from my driving. At this point, I was in first gear, going about five miles per hour.

I switched on the radio, and to my astonishment it was tuned to a station with perfect reception. The voice of Neil Diamond came booming through in the middle of a familiar refrain: "reaching out, touching you, touching meeeeee... Sweet Caroline!"

I was initially startled by the excellent reception. Then I remembered that it was supposed to be a message to me from Jesus, so I examined the words. I had been complaining that I couldn't receive the assurance that he was with me and here were words — along with a variant of my name — affirming that we were in contact. I was shocked and confused. "Is that song there for me?" I asked in wonder.

My body answered the question. Tears poured down my face, and energy blasted up my spine. There was absolutely no doubt in my mind that the answer was "Yes!" I believe that my guide, unable to reach my consciousness directly, had inspired some disc jockey to play that particular song on the station my radio was tuned to, and he had gotten me to turn it on at exactly the right moment to hear Jesus's message to me from the singer's mouth.

Laughing with relief, I confidently accelerated to a normal speed. It seemed ridiculous that a woman like me, born and bred in New York, could ever have been afraid of a little snow and ice. At the end of the ten-mile stretch to the free-way, I had already decided to continue on the secondary road through the mountains, but the authorities had closed the route over the pass due to heavy snow. I remember thinking a bit scornfully that they were probably being unnecessarily conservative. I was quite sure that I could have gotten through with no trouble if they would only let me try!

I find utterly preposterous the idea that the appearance of that particular phrase on my radio at that particular time was a "mere coincidence," and not just because it happened to me. I don't know what the odds are against a person named *Carolyn* desperately asking for reassurance about her inner teacher's presence who then hears an inner voice saying there will be a helpful message on the radio, switching on the radio to a station playing the exact words she wants most to hear, including a variant of her own name. Nevertheless, I'm quite certain that something like this would be expected to occur fewer than five times out of a hundred! My fellow psychologists would not ignore a pattern like this if it pertained to, say, discrimination learning in rats.

Things to Think About

1) Have you ever had an experience where it seemed like "Someone up there" was trying to tell you something? What did it feel like? What did you do?

2) We all know that some things are theoretically possible, but so unlikely that we can't bring ourselves to believe they could really have occurred by chance.

3) When coincidences are too meaningful, we tend to dismiss the idea that they are random events.

Chapter Six

Miracle Cures

'Tis as dangerous to be sentenced
by a Physician as a Judge.
— *Sir Thomas Brown*

In discussing miracles of deliverance from accidents and assaults, we've been confined to purely anecdotal evidence. Occurring suddenly and unpredictably, these incidents don't lend themselves to controlled experiments, replication, or even careful observation by objective third parties. However, the systematic study of divine intervention becomes marginally easier when the danger comes from illness, since many diseases tend to follow a predictable course over a period of months or years.

Investigations into alleged supernatural influences on disability and disease utilize a variety of approaches. There are, for example, retrospective studies of *spontaneous remissions*, where researchers try to identify the personal characteristics and the attitudinal and lifestyle changes that might have contributed to baffling recoveries. This approach closely resembles the one I've been taking with sudden reversals of fortune in cases of accidents and assaults. If we're on the right track, we'd expect to find evidence that the restoration of inner peace, and the decision to follow inner guidance, play prominent roles in unexpected healings as well.

Another approach to divine intervention in cases of illness involves the study of the effects of prayer. Investigators in this area attempt to learn whether — and under what conditions — the prayers of one person or group facilitate someone's recovery from disease or disability.

A third approach is the one taken by the medical commission studying alleged miracles at Lourdes. These physicians attempt to document spectacular cures attributed to spring water that is believed to have been imbued with healing properties by Mary, the mother of Jesus. The emphasis here is upon identifying cases where healing has been so sudden and complete that it seems that it *could not* have been caused by any known physical or psychological mechanism, and so it *must* therefore have been the result of divine intervention.

Those who study spontaneous remissions and their possible relationship to a person's lifestyle, beliefs, or attitudes are not necessarily committed to a belief in miracles, God, or the supernatural. While some believe in these things — holding that such changes reflect the sick person's determination to follow inner guidance, achieve inner peace, or open up to God's grace — others maintain that illnesses cured in this way must have been due to purely psychosomatic causes. In this view, if certain thoughts, attitudes, and behaviors predispose one to disease, changing them ought to reverse the process. Many believe that what appear to be miraculous healings actually represent nothing more than extreme examples of the ordinary — albeit poorly understood — interplay of the mind and body.

Investigators using any of these approaches must take into account certain variables, such as the healed person's faith in God, the healer, and/or the treatment. Many religious people believe that spiritual faith is instrumental in prompting God to act on one's behalf, but some scientists regard faith-based cures as examples of the *placebo effect*. It is well known that when patients believe they are being healed, they tend to improve regardless of the actual efficacy of the treatment. To determine whether divine intervention or the placebo effect is at work, researchers need to address such questions as: Can a faith healer heal someone who doesn't believe in faith healing? Will prayers benefit those who are unaware of being prayed for?

SPONTANEOUS REMISSION AND INNER PEACE

There have always been unexpected healings that physicians acknowledge could not have been caused by medical treatment alone. Historically, these have often been attributed to divine intervention, but modern doctors are more inclined to look to as-yet-unknown physical and psychological influences. In keeping with this approach, they refer to those who experience dramatic spontaneous remissions as "self-healers," implying that the answers will ultimately be found in the choices or actions of the individuals involved.

Cancer surgeon and writer Bernie Siegel facetiously observes that *spontaneous remission* is the accepted medical term for a miracle.[1] Nevertheless, no one really believes these cures are genuinely "spontaneous" in the sense of having no cause. As parapsychological investigator Stanley Krippner[2] points out, the term simply implies that we do not at present know what their cause might have been.

As we shall see, many physicians have observed that unexpected healings tend to be preceded by dramatic transformations in the individual's mental or spiritual outlook. Like people who experience deliverance from accidents and assaults, terminal patients who recover "spontaneously" appear, upon closer examination, to be actively doing something to produce their good fortune. As one woman who achieved a remission from lymphoma dryly remarked, "It wasn't spontaneous — I worked my ass off for it."[3]

In general, it isn't easy to determine if there is some particular mental state that tends to occur in connection with spontaneous remissions by looking at medical reports, since these usually omit all reference to the patient's state of mind. At most they might include a casual remark, such as this one about a woman considered beyond treatment with metastasized cervical cancer: "And her much hated husband suddenly died, whereupon she completely recovered."[4] A misguided allegiance to naturalism has too often led physicians to completely overlook the possibility that the patient's psychological or spiritual state *could* be affecting his or her health.

Some inexplicable healings — like that of the woman whose husband died — seem to have occurred because conditions in the sick individual's life became more congenial. A source of conflict was eliminated. Needed physical and emotional support became available. It would appear that these are cases where circumstances surrounding the sick person changed in such a way as to foster inner peace.

One could say the restoration of inner peace occurred by chance in these cases, but many other spontaneous remissions reflect a process of self-initiated change. Patients with terminal diagnoses sometimes set out to heal themselves by altering the beliefs and attitudes that produce negative emotions, such as fear, anger, depression, and guilt. There are even physicians who make the restoration of inner peace an integral part of their treatment.

Dr. Gerald Jampolsky, for example, founded the Center for Attitudinal Healing in Sausalito, California, an organization that provides support to catastrophically ill children and their families.[5] Patients are encouraged to work at recovering emotional equilibrium through loving and forgiving themselves and others. We have already seen that inner peace may be a precondition for miracles in cases of accidents and assaults. Might it also be a key to spontaneous remission?

THE MIRACLE-PRONE PERSONALITY

Although rigorous scientific research on this issue is lacking, there is some evidence to suggest that terminal patients who succeed in healing themselves do have some unusual characteristics. Indeed, *New Age Journal* editor Marc Barasch[6] proposed that there might actually be such a thing as a "miracle-prone personality."

First, many self-healers report that they went through some sort of *existential shift* before things began to improve. Sentenced to death, these individuals seem to search for the meaning of their lives. They take stock of their reasons for living and then reorganize their activities to focus upon what is really important to them.

For some, this inner shift leads to an abdication of onerous responsibilities in favor of *a more self-centered approach to life*. In the face of impending doom, self-healers seem to give themselves permission to finally do what they want rather than what they are "supposed" to do. This rejection of other people's expectations seems to free the individual to become immersed in activities and projects that are personally meaningful. As a result, they take a renewed interest in life and begin to feel they have something to live for.

Another attribute of people who achieve spontaneous remissions is a comfortable working relationship with reality. While some folks with terminal diagnoses simply deny the problem and go on with business as usual, those who achieve remissions do not kid themselves about the trouble they are in. They *accept their diagnoses* realistically and make necessary changes in their lifestyles.

And, while self-healers do not give up hope for a cure, being cured is often not their primary objective. They seem to place their main emphasis upon *living in a way that is congruent with their inner values* for as long as they have left.

From the point of view of our present inquiry into miracles, it is interesting that self-healers also frequently mention slipping into altered states of consciousness. They tend to be intuitive, hypnotizable, fantasy-prone individuals who find meaning in dreams and symbols and feel at home in their imaginations. In chapter 11, when we look more closely at the creative power of the mind, the significance of this will become apparent.

It is also intriguing that long-term survivors of terminal diagnoses tend to be rugged individualists who are both emotionally expressive and self-assertive. They don't necessarily follow medical advice to the letter, and — perhaps as a result — these argumentative, opinionated patients are often perceived rather negatively by their physicians. Medical descriptions of them frequently include terms such as *uncooperative, independent, bizarre, rebellious, antiauthoritarian*, and *nonconformist*.

If inner peace and continued hope are essential to accessing miracles, it may be that only highly independent people can maintain the necessary emotional equilibrium when faced with a damning diagnosis. For example, a doctoral student in Idaho who was researching spontaneous remission found that many of her subjects flatly refused to put much stock in the medical experts who had pronounced their death sentences. The researcher asked one woman, "How did you feel when the doctor told you that you had this terminal illness and that you'd be dead in six months?"

"That was *his* opinion," she replied tartly.

"Would you like to say more about that?" the interviewer prompted.

"Well, you know we're told all these things by all these experts. We live on a farm, and all these federal people come in and they look at the soil and they tell us that nothing will grow and we should put these fertilizers in and we should do all this stuff. We don't do it and hell, things grow there anyway. So why would I listen to an expert?"[7]

Given a choice between believing that she was doomed and believing that her doctor didn't have both oars in the water, this woman opted for the latter possibility. Further, notice the fearless quality of her thinking. This is not someone who is clinging to a physician as to a savior. She is not afraid to go it alone if necessary.

An "irrational" optimism in the face of a "hopeless" situation is yet another characteristic that people who achieve spontaneous remissions appear to share with those who experience miracles of deliverance from accidents and assaults. Sadly, some self-healers find it necessary to insulate themselves against medical skepticism in order to maintain this optimism.

For example, the Idaho researcher above quoted this reaction by a woman who had consented to be interviewed: "You're not a doctor, are you? I don't want to talk to a doctor!" The interviewer said, "No, I'm not. Really. Honest!" Then the woman replied, "Well, I just don't want to be put down and turned away again, like I was so many times. I'm going to keep my state of mind intact, no matter what!"[8]

We can readily understand how exposure to a physician's negative expectations might jeopardize a patient's inner peace, and therefore his or her remission. For example, one researcher was told by many of the long-term survivors he interviewed that their doctors had actually been *irritated* by their refusal to accept the hopelessness of their situations.[9]

Quite a few of these patients said that they had angrily walked out on their medical treatment. Their physicians never even knew that some of these "hopeless" cases recovered fully — much less *why* they did so.

However, even when patients with remissions do maintain medical contact, their doctors may be reluctant to credit their healings to something as intangible as prayer, a spiritual awakening, or a change of mental focus. In the case of my student Gino, for example, the attending physician did have an opportunity to learn that his patient had made an astonishing recovery, although, even then, he could not accept the idea that it could have resulted from the new thoughts Gino was entertaining.

GINO: NURSING HIS LIVER CELLS

At twenty-three, Gino nearly died of a serious illness. His condition was critical, and he had to spend weeks in the hospital and months in a convalescent facility until he stabilized and was able to go home. However, it would be too much to say that he had recovered. His life would never be the same.

It seems that an infection had destroyed most of Gino's liver. His doctor had had the unpleasant task of explaining to him that it would not regenerate itself. Gino's health would always be fragile, and for the rest of his life he would have to be hooked up to a machine that would do for him what his devastated liver could not.

With the disability money he received from the state, Gino was able to rent a tiny apartment. His many friends pitched in to do his shopping and cooking and to run his errands.

Bedridden and permanently attached by tubes to a machine that had to be wheeled along with him on trips to the bathroom, this once-athletic young man tried to keep his spirits up despite the knowledge that he was going to spend the rest of his life as an invalid.

Gino had a lot of time on his hands. In an effort to relieve his boredom, one of his friends brought him the book *Creative Visualization* by Shakti Gawain.[10] In it, Gawain described an ancient spiritual technique for changing reality. She said that you could actually heal yourself by altering the way you pictured things in your mind. Glad to fill his tedious days and sleepless nights with some constructive activity, Gino began to visualize the healing of his liver.

"I used to lie there and work on my liver one cell at a time," Gino told me years later. "It was just too damned depressing to focus on the whole thing at once. My liver appeared in my mind's eye like this big, black blob — all discolored and flabby with just this one little area of healthy pink tissue.

"So I would lie in bed imagining myself with a teensy-weensy little toothbrush, scrubbing the crud off of a single cell, rinsing it carefully, and gently massaging in magical medicines. I don't know that I seriously thought it was going to help, but it was something to do. There's just so much television a person can watch."

As the months wore on, Gino became a little stronger. He could move about the apartment more easily and prepare meals for himself. But he continued to fill his idle hours by mentally tending his liver cells. Sometimes when he was alone, he would even croon to them like a loving father, urging the "little guys" to take heart and heal themselves. And each day the liver in his visualization looked slightly improved. Little by little, there got to be more pink, healthy cells and fewer crud-encrusted, black ones.

One day as he was stepping out of his tiny kitchen, Gino caught his tubing on the edge of the counter. A sudden move on his part, and he felt agonizing pain as the plastic umbilicus was ripped out of his body. His doctor had warned that such an eventuality could be fatal, and Gino lost no time in phoning the paramedics.

Gino's doctor met him in the emergency room, looking grim. "I'll have to operate, but I want to do some tests first so I know where we stand. The nurse is going to take you down for some X-rays and stuff while I get scrubbed."

The tests were quickly completed, and Gino was prepped for surgery. After a short wait, however, the nurse returned and told him that something had gone wrong with his tests. They would have to be repeated.

Gino was put through another battery and was again left to wait. This time it was his doctor who appeared with an apologetic expression. These tests were no good either. How about one more round?

After the third battery was complete, Gino's doctor strode into his room and eyed him with speculation. He waved the sheaf of results in the air and demanded, "Where the hell did you get this liver?"

"What?" Gino replied weakly.

"This isn't your liver! I know your liver, and this isn't it!"

Gino was nonplussed. "What do you mean? What's wrong?" he asked.

"That's just it!" his physician exclaimed. "Nothing is wrong! There isn't a damn thing wrong with this liver. You left here five months ago with almost no liver function, and now you show up with this perfectly good liver. And what I want to know is — how the hell did you do that?"

"You're not going to believe this, Doc," Gino replied, "but it must have been the visualization I've been doing. For hours every day I've been visualizing my liver healing. I guess it did."

Gino was right about one thing. His doctor never did believe that the visualization could have worked such a miracle. Not that he had any other theories to explain how it could have happened!

When I knew Gino twenty years ago, when he was a graduate student in my class, he was a vital, energetic man in his thirties, with an unshakable belief in the power of mind over matter. This was what had led him to study psychology. As a psychotherapist, he hoped to help other people heal themselves by refocusing their thinking.

RESEARCH ON MIRACLES AT LOURDES

One of the few places where allegations of spontaneously occurring miracle cures have been carefully researched by qualified physicians is at the Shrine of the Virgin at Lourdes, France. That's where a spring is believed to have emerged from the spot on which the Virgin Mary is said to have appeared to a fourteen-year-old girl named Bernadette Soubirous in 1858. Since then, millions of people from around the world have made the pilgrimage to Lourdes hoping for miraculous healing, and large numbers of them assert that they received the help they sought. Records of cures associated with Lourdes have been kept since the first healing was reported while the Marian apparitions were still going on in 1858. However, in 1947 the Catholic Church formally established an international medical team to thoroughly investigate the claims of miraculous healing.

The procedure is as follows:[11] When a pilgrim reports a sudden cure, he or she is interviewed and examined by the physician on duty in the sanctuary. If the case seems to meet the committee's criteria — that it be a final and definite cure of a dire condition, occurring with "supernatural" rapidity — the physician convenes a medical board involving any medical doctors, of whatever religion, who happen to be present in the sanctuary that day and are willing to participate.

If the case is deemed "medically inexplicable" by the medical board, the physician follows the patient's progress for at least three years before deciding whether to submit a report to the International Medical Committee of Lourdes. This committee currently has twenty permanent members — all distinguished physicians — some Catholic, some of other religions, and even a few who are agnostics or atheists. Additionally, the committee consults with some ten thousand adjunct members representing more than seventy nations and a wide variety of beliefs, including agnostics and atheists.

One of the permanent members is assigned the case and charged with investigating it thoroughly, reading all of the current medical literature in that area and consulting with other physicians and scientists as necessary. He or she prepares a report to be discussed at the committee's annual meeting. The full committee then tries to determine whether "the cure of this person constitutes a phenomenon which is contrary to the observations and expectations of medical knowledge, and is inexplicable according to present scientific knowledge."

If a two-thirds majority of the permanent members believes the case to be a candidate for a miracle, the healed individual's local bishop convenes a committee of local physicians who consider the case further, interviewing friends and relatives of the person alleging the miracle and taking into account current developments in the person's condition. In the end, the local bishop is the one who decides whether to declare the cure "miraculous." Of more than six thousand cases where miracles have been alleged, some sixty-five have presently been accepted as actual miracles.

VITTORIO MICHELLI: A MIRACLE AT LOURDES

In 1962, Vittorio Michelli's hip joint was completely destroyed by cancer (specifically, a fusiform-cell carcinoma). The pelvis was disintegrated, and the leg was nearly separated. He was treated in the military hospital at Trente, Italy, where the destructive progress of the disease was charted with radiological evidence.

A year after his initial diagnosis, Michelli went to Lourdes and was bathed in the waters in the plaster cast that was holding his hip together. He reported sudden sensations of heat moving through his body while he was in the water, and when he emerged from the spring, his appetite and energy returned immediately. A month later, his doctors finally consented to remove the cast and take another X-ray. When they did so, they determined that the tumor was regressing.

The tumor soon disappeared completely, at which point the bone began to regrow and eventually completely reconstructed the hip. Michelli was walking two months after his return from Lourdes. Brendan O'Regan of the Institute of Noetic Sciences quotes the committee's report to this effect: "A completely destroyed articulation was completely reconstructed without any surgical intervention. The lower limb which was useless became sound, the prognosis is indisputable, the patient is alive and in a flourishing state of health nine years after his return from Lourdes."[12] The committee's report on Michelli also stated: "A remarkable reconstruction of the iliac bone and cavity has taken place. The X-rays made in 1964, 1965, 1968 and 1969 confirm categorically and without doubt that an unforeseen, and even overwhelming bone reconstruction has taken place, of a type unknown in the annals of world medicine."

Dissenting Opinions

While a story like the one above certainly seems authentically miraculous, some cases deemed "medically inexplicable" by the International Medical Committee of Lourdes, and "miraculous" by the Catholic Church, have proven less convincing to independent investigators. British psychologist Donald West, for example, points out that most of these miracle cures involve diseases such as cancer and tuberculosis that are known to be extremely susceptible to psychosomatic

influences. He believes that the positive expectations generated in believers by the visit to Lourdes might well have been
enough to reverse the courses of these diseases in the absence
of any divine intervention.[13]

Other physicians suggest that several cures probably represent cases where multiple sclerosis was misdiagnosed as
some other disorder. The sudden disappearance of symptoms
is much less amazing if this is so, since it is well known that
the course of MS often involves dramatic spontaneous remissions.[14] Then, too, a 1963 miraculous cure of Budd-Chiari
Syndrome is called into question by the fact that seven years
later the "healed" woman did, in fact, die of that disease.[15]

Research of the kind done at Lourdes inevitably gives
rise to conflicting findings and interpretations. Unfortunately, those of us considering the disparate views of experts
working from very different assumptions are seldom in a position to independently evaluate their claims. Should we
trust the diagnoses agreed upon by the many physicians who
actually examined these patients, or the speculations of later,
albeit possibly more knowledgeable, doctors who suspect
that the attending physicians all got it wrong?

Further, where does psychosomatic influence end and divine intervention, if it exists, begin? Most medical practitioners today would have no trouble accepting the idea that a
dramatic change in Michelli's thinking could have cured his
cancer. But could it be responsible for regrowing his hip, or
must we resort to divine intervention to account for that extraordinary development? Where one expert says one thing
and another disagrees, we are left to make our own choice
about which one to believe.

I believe the literature on spontaneous remission supports the idea that, like people snatched from death through accidents and assaults, those who are healed of "terminal" conditions change their thinking, follow their inner promptings, and adjust their lifestyles in ways that nurture inner peace. In chapter 8 we'll look more closely at the life-or-death importance of one's state of mind.

Things to Think About

1) Like those who receive miracles in cases of accidents and assaults, people who achieve spontaneous remissions cultivate inner peace.

2) Self-healers also seem to become more inner-directed, changing their lives to focus on what is truly important and meaningful to them. Do you think divine guidance could be playing a role here?

3) The attribution of a healing to a miracle always involves personal judgment. What would it take to convince you that a healing was miraculous?

Chapter Seven

The Healing Effects of Prayer

Miracles arise from a mind that is ready for them.

— *A Course in Miracles*

*I*t seems clear that our own thoughts can have a profound effect upon the health of our bodies. Few, if any, modern physicians would disagree with this. But what about the thoughts of others? Can the good wishes of others — in the form of prayers — heal us?

THE PLACEBO EFFECT

As mentioned in the last chapter, one problem in evaluating the efficacy of prayer is the need to distinguish the influence of prayer itself from that of the placebo effect of faith. In medicine, a placebo is an inert substance or treatment administered to a sick person who is led to believe that it will have a beneficial effect upon her or his condition. Sometimes when this is done, the sick person gets better, even though no actual medicine was administered. Where the effect of prayer is concerned, a patient's faith in God, or in the people doing the praying, can produce very positive expectations that have a powerful healing effect of their own. Often it's hard to tell whether it was the prayer itself or the positive expectations it generated that caused the person to heal.

To separate out the placebo effect, researchers testing the efficacy of new drugs and therapies generally compare the results obtained by an experimental group — which receives what the investigators hope will turn out to be an effective medicine or healing intervention — to the progress of a similarly ill group whose members *believe* they are receiving the new treatment but are not. The placebo group's results allow researchers to evaluate the effects of the treatment against those produced by the patient's positive expectations alone.

A well-known example of the power of the placebo effect concerns a patient treated by the distinguished psychologist Bruno Klopfer in 1957 at UCLA.[1] Mr. Wright was in the terminal stage of cancer when he learned that a new drug called Krebiozen — touted in the press as a miracle cure for cancer — was being tested at the facility where he was receiving treatment. He begged to be given the drug, and since it was Friday and his patient was not expected to survive the weekend, Klopfer administered a single shot of Krebiozen out of compassion for the dying man. He returned Monday morning expecting to hear that Mr. Wright had died, only to find his patient walking around the ward eagerly telling everyone the good news that his tumors — which had been the size of oranges on Friday — were now half their size. He was discharged ten days later in complete remission.

However, reports that Krebiozen had been clinically tested and found to be worthless began appearing in the press. Upon becoming convinced that the drug *could not* have helped him, the man found his tumors coming back.

Dr. Klopfer realized that it had actually been this man's faith in Krebiozen as a "miracle" drug that had cured him, so Klopfer told the patient that he had access to a still newer and much more powerful form of the medication. It had only just now become available for clinical testing, he explained, but it really did work wonders. He injected the man with water, and as before the tumors immediately began to regress. By the end of his course of water injections, the patient was once again symptom-free for a number of months.

Unfortunately, the news subsequently surfaced that it had now been definitively proven that all forms of Krebiozen were worthless in treating cancer. Realizing that this must be so, Klopfer's patient once again began regrowing his tumors and soon died.

As you can see, the therapeutic effect of a patient's positive expectations can be so powerful that it's hard to know when, or indeed whether, it is ever necessary to invoke divine intervention as an explanation for sudden and dramatic healings. It's clear that something about the belief that one will be healed can activate little-understood healing mechanisms within the body. Yet, as far as most investigators are concerned, if a healing is to be regarded as miraculous, it must be demonstrated that something occurred that could not be accounted for by the patient's positive expectations alone.

PRAYER VERSUS THE PLACEBO EFFECT OF FAITH

One way to separate the effects of prayer from those of the patient's positive expectations is to observe what happens when sick people are prayed for without their knowledge. In 1988, scientific interest in the healing effects of prayer was triggered by the surprising results of a study at a San Francisco coronary care unit.[2] At the time of admission to the unit, patients were randomly assigned to either a control group that received medical treatment alone or an experimental group whose members received comparable medical care but were also being prayed for by volunteers without the knowledge of patients or staff.

Results indicated that the prayed-for patients had significantly fewer complications, required only a fifth of the antibiotics needed by the control group, and were only a third as likely to develop pulmonary swelling. Since neither the staff nor the patients knew about the prayer variable, there should not have been any placebo effect involved in these results.

A subsequent study at Duke University Medical Center[3] assigned 150 heart patients to the following groups: 1) a control group receiving medical treatment alone; 2) medical treatment plus touch therapy; 3) medical treatment plus relaxation training; 4) medical treatment plus guided imagery lessons; and 5) medical treatment plus being prayed for without their knowledge. All of the groups who received something more than medical treatment alone were 25 to 30 percent less likely to experience complications than members of the medical-treatment-only group. However, those being prayed for without their knowledge had the lowest rate of complications of any of the groups.

Here, the placebo effect should have been present for all groups except the no-additional-treatment control group and the prayed-for one. The fact that the prayed-for patients' results were significantly better than those of the other additional-treatment groups suggests that prayer added some healing influence that the placebo effect — and whatever effects the other additional treatments provided — didn't.

Studies like the ones above, where patients are prayed for without their knowledge, suggest that the healing effects of prayer are not limited to the placebo effect. According to a review of research on prayer and healing by Daniel J. Benor, "there is highly significant evidence for healing effects on enzymes, cells in the laboratory, bacteria, yeasts, plants, animals and humans."[4]

Are We Testing for God's Influence, or Testing God?

These experiments — where an independent variable is manipulated, potentially confounding variables are randomized or controlled, and results are subjected to standard statistical tests — have the trappings of sound scientific methodology. But upon closer inspection, it isn't clear how we should interpret their findings. When prayer is your independent variable, you quickly find yourself in deep water.

First, if we are assuming that God is intervening to heal the members of the prayed-for group but not the members of the control group, why are the prayed-for subjects only *somewhat improved*, relative to controls? Why aren't they cured? If God were going to go to the trouble of getting involved in the first place, couldn't He or She manage more than "significant improvement" — and even that, only on some measures but not others? If actual divine intervention were involved, surely we'd be entitled to expect something more than this.

But the difficulties in interpreting the research on prayer and healing go even deeper. Let's imagine that we eventually find some formula for invoking divine intervention that is consistently effective. Say, for instance, that we get ten volunteers to recite a particular prayer a certain number of times a day for a certain number of days. And let's say we find that in response to those prayers, the people prayed for are all healed.

What would that say about the nature of God? As several physicians involved in prayer research point out, it certainly sounds as if we would have found a way to *compel God to do our will.*[5] Is such a thing possible? Is it desirable? Should we be putting God to the test in this way — tempting God to prove His or Her existence and power? Certainly the Bible deems this a no-no (Exodus 17:7; Luke 4:12). And what happens to the idea that we are here to do *God's* will?

For these and many other reasons, some researchers suggest that it is simply not possible to evaluate supernatural phenomena by the same standards as natural ones. I think they're right. Even providing an operational definition of *prayer*, or establishing the construct validity of the concept, presents serious, and quite possibly insurmountable, problems.[6]

Maybe that's why some who investigate the healing effects of prayer leave God out of the equation. Instead of conceptualizing prayer as a request for help from a supernatural being, they focus on the possibility that its healing effects are produced by the transfer of a subtle healing energy from the individual praying to the recipient of the prayer. Others hypothesize that prayer initiates some sort of telepathic communication whereby the person praying influences the mind of the patient to heal her or his own body. This raises interesting issues itself.

HEALING PRAYER AS A NATURAL, NOT A SUPERNATURAL, PHENOMENON

How is it possible that the prayers of others could influence the health of folks they've never met — ones who don't even consciously realize they are being prayed for? After all, if the mind were nothing more than an illusory sense of self produced by the chemical and electrical activity of the brain, there would be no way for thoughts to affect anything at all, and certainly nothing beyond one's own body. If God were not involved, is there any reason to think that prayer could nonetheless affect the prayed-for individual directly? Can thoughts (prayers) influence the behavior of material things (bodies)?

When someone uses mental power in an effort to influence the behavior of physical objects (such as dice, a random number generator, etc.), it's called *psychokinesis*. When the emphasis is upon making things turn out well for others, it's called *intentional healing* or *prayer*. More than a decade of experimentation at Princeton University's PEAR (Princeton Engineering Anomalies Research) program and elsewhere has produced "unmistakable statistical evidence" that people *can* influence physical processes at a distance through the intention to do so.[7]

In 1989, for example, one researcher[8] collected all of the published studies concerned with efforts to mentally influence the fall of dice. Analyzing all of these results together, he found a small but highly consistent experimental effect indicating that psycho-kinesis is real. The possibility that an effect of this magnitude could have been due to chance was calculated to be on the order of a *billion to one*. In 1991, another study[9] analyzed results from thirty-seven experiments where subjects were asked to try to mentally influence various physiological response systems of distant volunteers, such as blood pressure or muscle tremor. The positive results were so significant that the odds they could have occurred by chance were *one in a hundred trillion*.

It's no longer possible to duck the conclusion that the mind is real, and that it can influence the behavior of material things, including the condition of one's own body and the bodies of distant individuals. According to Dr. Larry Dossey[10] of the Panel on Mind/Body Interventions at the National Institutes of Health, current research is showing that the mind is "nonlocal." This is to say that it behaves in the laboratory as though it is *omnipresent* and exists *independent of the brain* through which it operates. Indeed, it's beginning to look like the human mind is itself a supernatural phenomenon — as it should be if we are truly created "in the image and likeness" of God.

So yes, it is possible that prayers could help heal another person in the absence of any divine intervention. Next, we'll explore a theory of healing that will begin to answer some of the questions we've raised about miracles.

Things to Think About

1) Your thoughts can influence other people and things at a distance.

2) Your thoughts exert a powerful influence over the health of your body.

3) Science is never going to shed much light on the mechanisms of prayer — only your own personal experiments will solve this mystery.

Chapter Eight

How Miracles of Healing Are Created

The body is endangered by the mind that hurts itself.
— *A Course in Miracles*

*H*ere is another story of a miraculous healing — one in which the doctor played an integral, active, and supportive role. It is a clear, detailed example of everything we've discussed so far, and we can use it to try to figure out how it is that miracles work. I met Christine and her physician when we appeared together on a TV talk show some years ago. The quotes below are taken from the notes of the production assistant who interviewed them before the program.

CHRISTINE: A MIRACULOUS HEALING

In August 1989, Christine was diagnosed with breast cancer. She underwent a radical mastectomy in September, followed by three rounds of aggressive chemotherapy, but by December she was worse. Just before Christmas, she was rushed to the hospital with pneumonia, and it was discovered that the cancer had metastasized to her lungs.

At that point, Christine's cancer specialist, Dr. Jeffrey Scott, was compelled to admit that her prospects were grim. "It's the worst prognosis if someone is getting the best therapy and the cancer comes back. And the lungs are a very bad place for it to come back to. Then it really predicts for doing poorly." He estimated that this patient had less than six months to live.

At Dr. Scott's suggestion, Christine sought a second opinion. However, the new doctor told her she was likely to be dead within three or four months. It was time for Christine to put her affairs in order and make some arrangements for her eight-year-old daughter, Rachel.

Throughout the dismal process of diagnosis and treatment, this dying woman had been tormented by worry about her child. Christine knew all too well what it felt like to lose one's family. Except for her daughter, she was alone in the world herself, and she could not bear the thought of leaving Rachel in that position. So great was her distress over this that Dr. Scott began to suspect that her emotional turmoil might be interfering with her response to treatment.

"Christine and I got very close," Dr. Scott reported. "I knew her mother had just died, and that she didn't have any family members that she could feel comfortable leaving Rachel with." One night Dr. Scott discussed his patient's painful dilemma with his wife. The next day this generous man assured Christine that when she died, he and his wife would adopt Rachel and raise her as their own.

"I want to emphasize that we were talking about 'when' she died — not 'if,'" Scott added. "I thought aggressive chemotherapy might prolong Christine's life, but there was really no question of her getting well again. I never tell anyone that they are going to die unless there is no alternative, but we had to be frank because she had Rachel, and she had to know the score."

Christine's mind was more at ease now that her physician had promised to provide a loving home for Rachel, but she still could not bear the thought of what her daughter would go through in losing her only parent. Casting about for anything she might try as a last resort, Christine remembered a passage from the Bible that says that if people are ill, the elders of the church should be assembled to pray for them. Since medicine could offer her no hope of a cure, Christine asked the minister of her church if he and some of the other parishioners would assemble and pray for a miracle.

"I grew up Pentecostal," Christine explained, "but I'm a Southern Baptist now, and they don't usually do that. But my minister is a good man, and he said 'yes.' He got some of the deacons together, and some of my friends were there, too. One week before they prayed for me, tests showed that I was covered with cancer."

Dr. Scott supported Christine in her decision to seek miraculous healing, although he insisted that she continue her medical treatment as well. "I know that miracles occur," he told her, "but they don't happen every time. It's important that we use every tool we have."

Christine was in complete agreement. "I knew that God could heal me, but that I had to use my head, too. God gives you a brain to work with, and he also guides Dr. Scott's hand."

The members of her congregation had never done anything quite like this before, but under their minister's guidance they willingly gathered to ask God to heal their friend. However, despite their best efforts, Christine had to admit that she did not feel any dramatic change in her condition as a result of the prayer meeting.

A few days later, Christine celebrated a birthday everyone assumed would be her last. The friends who gathered to share this bittersweet occasion presented her with a beautiful cake ablaze with thirty-eight lighted candles. It was time to make a wish and blow them out.

"All I could think about was Rachel," Christine said. "I closed my eyes and made a wish that I would be free of cancer, so that I could be there for her as she grew up." Then this woman who was recovering from pneumonia, and supposedly dying of lung cancer, drew in a mighty breath and effortlessly blew out every one of the thirty-eight candles!

"I knew that it was a sign from God," Christine laughed. "I must have been healed, or I couldn't have done it. I arranged for a lung scan, and sure enough, my cancer was completely gone!"

Asked what his reaction had been to the discovery that the lung cancer had disappeared, Dr. Scott exclaimed, "Shock! I thought we must have made a mistake. Maybe the breast cancer hadn't really metastasized to the lungs, and somehow it had just been the pneumonia we had been seeing. But we looked back at the biopsy, and it hadn't been a mistake. There's no question that Christine really had advanced, metastatic lung cancer, and there's no doubt that it had completely disappeared a week after she was prayed for.

"I can't explain why she is still here and well four and a half years later," he went on. "If it's a miracle, I don't care, because I'm thrilled. I believe in God, and as a physician I know that things happen that we can't explain."

Christine followed through on her medical treatment, despite the fact that there was no longer any trace of the cancer. Three years later, Dr. Scott had the pleasure of walking his former patient down the aisle, as he gave her away to a new husband. She attributes her healing to a miracle, jointly performed by the members of her church and her beloved friend and cancer specialist, Dr. Jeffrey Scott.

Christine's healing raises any number of interesting questions. Did God intervene to heal her in response to the prayers of her fellow parishioners? Might the group's loving thoughts have effected the healing without any divine intervention? Or is it possible that Christine's positive expectations actually did the job?

Further, if this was an instance of divine intervention, why didn't God act until others prayed for her? Surely Christine must have prayed for herself. Why weren't her prayers enough?

As you can see, even if we grant that prayer works, we're still left to figure out what causes it to work, and why it works in some cases and not others. Is it about the attitude of the patient, the number of people praying for her, or the frequency, kind, or intensity of their prayers? Is a positive result more or less likely depending upon whether we pray for the restoration of health or that God's will be done? As impressive as the healing in Christine's case is, we're going to have to work at understanding how it was achieved.

Miracle-Mindedness Is the Key

In the previous chapter we looked at studies that seemed to show that the loving intentions of one person can influence the health of another; if you pray for someone who is sick, it may help them get better. However, the healing effects in the studies seemed rather weak and gradual — more a matter of somewhat lowered blood pressure, or a small, but statistically significant degree of pain reduction. This is quite different from the kind of rapid and complete healing that we find in the stories of Christine and Vittorio.

This leads me to suspect that there are two types of healing involving prayer. The first is weaker, and it is probably produced by the transmission of energy and/or positive mental suggestions from one person to another, or by the sick individual's concentration upon positive thoughts. The second, very strong effect occurs when the person involved becomes fully "miracle-minded," becoming open and welcoming to actual divine intervention. I think that sometimes the first kind of prayer is necessary to prepare the sick person to accept or engage in the second kind.

In discussing miracles in cases of accidents and assaults, I suggested that there were things endangered individuals had to do in order to permit divine intervention. At a *minimum*, these people had to abandon fear and anger and retreat into a detached, peaceful, and unconditionally loving state of higher consciousness. I've previously referred to this state of mind as *meditation*, but now I'm going to further identify it as the state *A Course in Miracles* calls *miracle-mindedness*. I believe that a person must achieve miracle-mindedness in order to experience divine intervention, and that one who hopes to perform miracles for others — by praying for them, performing the laying on of hands, and so on — must be miracle-minded as well.

How does our own state of mind affect that of another person? *A Course in Miracles* says that we constantly broadcast our thoughts at a psychic level, and that as a result, we are all immersed in an invisible sea of thoughts emitted by others. This means that a mind that is worried, resentful, or preoccupied automatically projects its unsettling perspective, bombarding others with ideas that tend to provoke anxiety, depression, and irritability. Alternatively, when a person is resting in peace and joy and is confident that everything is going to turn out fine, his or her mind offers this perspective to others, and especially to anyone about whom the person is thinking. Perhaps you've noticed the way people around you tend to match consciousness with you. If you're in a bad mood, others are likely to become irritable and uncooperative in your presence. Alternatively, when you're in love, total strangers go out of their way to be charming and helpful.

The *Course* goes on to say that while we are all subconsciously aware of the thoughts of others, these thoughts affect us very little unless we *agree* with them. Nevertheless, the more people who already believe in a particular idea, and thus project it to others, the more persuasive that idea becomes to everyone else. In the extreme, this results in the formation of a *consensual illusion*, where the vast majority of people within a given culture accept certain beliefs — for instance, about the role of women, or the way children should be brought up — without question as things that "everybody knows." There is a lot of pressure to accept and conform to such widely held beliefs, and only very independent thinkers dare to question them.

The ideas we pick up from others and adopt as our own influence the way we perceive ourselves, our bodies, other people, and the world. In this way, each of us creates for ourselves a unique worldview based upon the things we've chosen to believe. This amounts to a *personal illusion* — one that the mystics of many religions say causes us to anticipate, and therefore experience, only the things we are prepared to believe could really happen in "our" world. Think, for example, of Kathleen, who was prepared to believe she could be raped, but utterly unwilling to believe she would be killed.

In chapters 10 and 11, we'll explore further how the power of belief generates what we take to be "reality," but for now, I just want to focus on one of its implications: That in order to experience harm through an illness, attack, or accident, we must first believe that someone or something can affect us against our will. This means that a person who absolutely refuses to believe he can be injured in a particular situation can't be. The rules of his personal illusion simply make no provision for such a thing to occur.

I believe that when endangered individuals slip away from the turmoil and preconceptions of their everyday ego consciousness and into miracle-mindedness — which is to say, when they reidentify with the aspect of their minds they share with God and all other beings — they leave their personal illusions behind and experience actual reality, as God is Being It. The *Course* says that beneath the illusions with which we ordinarily distort our perceptions lies the eternally loving movement of God, which constitutes the "real world."

In a totally peaceful, undefended mental state, we are in a position to remember and reexperience the truth that God created all of us eternal and invulnerable, and that we are only dreaming that it is possible for anything to happen to us against our will. Certainly those of us who have forgotten that we are part of God can and do imagine we are at the mercy of forces beyond our control. But a mind at rest in a state of miracle-mindedness sees this to be absurd. This realization that our own will is more powerful than any circumstance we might carelessly have dreamed up leads to a deep sense of inner peace, as well as to boundless compassion for all of our brothers and sisters who are still thrashing around in their own illusory nightmares.

Like someone becoming lucid within a bad dream, I believe that a miracle-minded individual abandons her or his personal illusion in order to see all things as God intends them to be seen: through the eyes of love. Love quite literally dissolves illusion. In any situation looked upon with unconditional love, whatever is illusory disappears, and all that remains to be seen is the wholly benevolent divine reality God is Being, right there where something dangerous or unfair appears to be occurring.

When we yield to love in this way, we stop projecting fear at both a conscious and an unconscious level. At the same time, we release our commitment to our belief that we are helpless and victimized, and this allows something new and unexpected to occur in our experience. And since we are communicating only love, the whole world responds lovingly. Perhaps a now-you-see-him-now-you-don't lifeguard appears to tow us to shore, or an eleventh-hour beaver pond materializes to cushion our fall. People pray for us and our cancer disappears. Serial killers about to take our lives undergo a sudden and totally uncharacteristic change of heart. We dream we are in no real danger, and sure enough, suddenly we aren't.

True, from the point of view of ordinary ego consciousness, some of the endings achieved when people slip into miracle-mindedness are so absurdly implausible that no self-respecting editor would allow them in a work of fiction. Yet it is always our ego's frightening illusions that are the real fiction. God is creating nothing that can harm the Children of God. Divine reality is totally safe and unfailingly kind to everyone. That's why we call it *Heaven*.

Further, while it is these dramatic positive reversals of fortune that we ordinarily think of as miracles, *A Course in Miracles* says that it's the shift in perception from ordinary ego-consciousness to miracle-mindedness that is the real miracle. This shift instantly relieves the suffering of the miracle-minded individual, even on those occasions when it does not produce any noticeable change in her or his physical circumstances. Your son, for example, may continue to be a drug addict, but in a state of miracle-mindedness, you'll find a way to be at peace with the situation and no longer torment yourself over it, or make it worse through your own misguided efforts to compel him to change.

THE ROLE OF GOD AND PRAYER IN MIRACLES

God is Love. The moment we enter that peaceful, meditative state, we recognize that we are under no law but God's, and we abandon the belief that illusions have the power to threaten us. Instantly, as a direct result of our refusal to believe anything can hurt us, it becomes true in our experience, and events take whatever turn is necessary to dispel the illusion of danger.

This insight is actually part of our folk wisdom, reflected in sayings about Heaven protecting "fools" (meaning those who don't have the intellectual capacity to realize how dangerous everyone else thinks a situation really is), and ones that suggest it's always the fool who doesn't realize something can't be done who goes ahead and does it. Our limiting beliefs about what is possible actually limit what we can experience.

When we enter miracle-mindedness, we release all limiting beliefs, and this allows the divine Presence within us to help us revise our ongoing waking dream for the better. The result is a change in perspective that changes our role in any ongoing interaction. We cease to see ourselves as the victim of circumstances beyond our control and discover we are not helpless. We stop believing our disease is incurable, and find it cured. We refuse any longer to believe death is inevitable just because we've driven off a cliff or are drowning, and sure enough, circumstances rearrange themselves in such a way as to prove us right.

What is the nature of the supernatural force that intervenes when we become miracle-minded? It is my belief that God does not intervene in our affairs directly. Our Creator bestowed free will upon us and imbued our minds with divinity — the power to create the experiences we can bring ourselves to believe possible, whether those experiences are sudden wealth, a happy relationship, an assault, an accident, or a deadly disease. God knows that we are only dreaming the experiences that seem to menace us, and that when we become genuinely disenchanted with our nightmares, we'll wake up and realize that we've been safe in reality (Heaven) all the time we were dreaming up illusory terrors. In the meantime, as long as our ego's drama holds some attraction for us, we are free to slug it out with the "cruel world" we are making up and granting the power to thwart us.

Miracle-mindedness is thus the universal, God-given remedy for everything that ails us. Divine intervention — which is to say, *intervention by the divine aspect of our very own minds* — becomes possible whenever we realize that we are only imagining the world we seem to see around us, and that we are free to imagine it differently. *Our minds* are extensions of the Mind of God, and as such, they are *supernatural*. But, like Dorothy in Oz, we don't know to call upon the "magical" powers of our "ruby slippers" until we realize that that power is there.

It is always ultimately our own mind that heals us, just as it was our own mind that caused our illness. The prayers of others don't directly heal or rescue us. If they could, it would mean that someone else would have power over us and could deprive us of the fruits of our chosen beliefs — against our will, even if "for our own good." Besides, if someone could take away a sickness we'd created through misthought, couldn't they just as easily use their power over us for "evil" and cast spells to make us sick?

But this is not to say that the prayers of others play no role at all in healing. I believe that effective prayer is a matter of one mind encouraging another to relax into the state of inner peace that makes miraculous reversals of fortune possible. At a psychic level, miracle-minded individuals inspire others to retreat from ego-generated conflicts into the peace and power of their own right minds. Unfortunately, not everyone who says a prayer takes the additional step of becoming miracle-minded before doing so.

For example, if some of the friends who prayed for Christine were worried about her, distressed by her physical deterioration, or afraid they'd fail her, the actual thoughts they would have been offering her to identify with would not have provided much benefit, despite their good intentions. Indeed, to whatever extent she was influenced to agree with their fears, such prayers would only have made it harder for her to find her way to peace and healing. On the other hand, those who were embracing Christine in serenity, unconditional love, and the confidence that she really could get well would have tended to draw her into her own right mind where a miracle would become possible. This confidence is often called *faith*, but I believe it is actually *knowledge* — the knowledge that anyone can reverse a bad situation at any time by releasing judgment and retreating into peace and love.

The Role of Miracle Workers — And How to Become One

The prayers of some people — those who know the power of their own minds and are peacefully confident that miracles are always possible — are exceptionally effective in encouraging miracle-mindedness in others, along with the dramatic physical healings that often ensue. We tend to call these people *healers*, or *miracle workers*, although only those individuals they are able to persuade to enter a state of miracle-mindedness are actually healed.

At a large prayer service or tent show, for instance, it's likely that there will be at least one person present who is miracle-minded, even if it isn't the one conducting the service. That lone healer, whoever he or she might be, is available to support the tentative willingness of many others to slip into their own right minds and heal themselves if that is truly what they came there to do. But then so are the minds of all of the awakened children of God and all of the miracle-minded individuals on this planet or elsewhere in the universe. People who are willing to be drawn into miracle-mindedness have no shortage of models to encourage and guide them.

This, I believe, is yet another reason why researching prayer is so problematic. A single loving thought by a miracle-minded stranger could conceivably induce miracle-mindedness in a sick or otherwise endangered individual, while millions praying from their wrong minds (from their egos) may have little or no beneficial effect. And no matter how many would-be miracle workers are beaming love from a peaceful state of miracle-mindedness, there is no guarantee that the person being prayed for will accept the suggestion. People have free will, and if they prefer to obsess about their problems, dramatize their sufferings, cherish resentments, or seek some collateral advantage through their pain, they are free to do so. Even great healers can't help those who are unwilling to release their problem to solution.

If we want to help someone achieve a miracle, we'd be

wise to encourage that person's miracle-mindedness by being miracle-minded ourselves. We should also do whatever we can to help her or him feel safe, hopeful, and at peace. Anything that promotes relaxation, positive expectations, and enjoyment is a step in the right direction. This could involve activities as varied as sending patients loving thoughts from a state of inner peace, verbally assuring them of our love and support, taking them to a healing shrine or prayer meeting, lighting a candle for them, convincing superstitious individuals that you've removed a curse that has been afflicting them, or, in the case of a physician, administering a substance they believe to be a beneficial drug. Christine's doctor, for example, sensed that her distress over the fate of her daughter was interfering with her response to treatment. Once he was able to assure his patient that Rachel would be lovingly cared for in his own family, it seems likely that Christine was able to relax for the first time since her diagnosis.

I suspect that this release from worry greatly facilitated her entry into a peaceful state of miracle-mindedness. Indeed, coupled with the outpouring of love Christine received at her prayer service and birthday party, it seems to have done the trick. She momentarily forgot her troubles and slipped back into her right mind. There, the divine truth that as a Child of God she *could not be at the mercy of a disease* — unless she preferred to believe she could be — evidently dawned upon her. Once she became miracle-minded, the thought that a Child of God could have something to fear from cancer was no longer being invested with belief, and her illness vanished.

This is not to say that Christine or Vittorio, or anyone else who creates miracles, is aware of thinking, "I have nothing to fear from this." It is more a peaceful sense of being "bigger" than your problem and unafraid of the future. It's a conviction that everything is going to be all right, despite every depressing thing you think you know about the situation.

YOUR DIVINE GUIDE

Many religions describe the existence of divine guides, which are variously called guardian angels, patron saints, ancestors, gurus, power animals, muses, the Holy Spirit, or Shekinah, the personal aspect of God. *A Course in Miracles* says that our inner guide shares the Mind of God with us and is always available to show us how to use the supernatural power of our own minds to keep ourselves safe and satisfied, as God intends. These divine guides are, I believe, our awakened brothers and sisters sent by God to comfort us as we dream and to help us reawaken to our divinity when we are ready to do so.

As we shall see, the ego is the aspect of the mind that generates illusions. As awakened (enlightened, self-realized, Christ-like, Buddha-like) beings, our guides have no egos, and thus, no personal or consensual illusions. They are present with us in our minds throughout our lives, and they commune with us whenever we turn away from our ordinary thought processes to listen. They are there to give us good advice and, with our permission, to protect us and act on our behalf behind the scenes. But they are not authorized by God to interfere in our dreams without our permission. If we want their help, we must turn the situation over to them.

I believe we "turn the situation over to our higher power"

and authorize our guides to help us by entering miracle-mindedness. It's a little like a tag-team match in professional wrestling. If you want your partner to take over for you, you've got to go to where he or she stands reaching out to you from outside the ring and make contact. Some spectators will be encouraging a badly beaten contestant to make the tag, and others — who want him to lose — will encourage him to focus on his opponent instead of seeking help from his partner. I'm on your side, so I'm encouraging you to tag your guide and enlist her or his remarkable abilities to protect you and to show you how to use the supernatural power of your own mind to keep yourself safe.

When someone is in need of a miracle, and prepared to consider miracle-mindedness as a solution, I believe her or his guide prompts other individuals who are currently miracle-minded to pray for her or him. That's what I believe happened to Christine and her supporters. I think it is also what happened to Louis and me.

LOU: EXPLOITING A WINDOW OF MIRACLE-READINESS

In the mid-1980s, well before the advent of modern AIDS medicine, I became concerned about a friend who had AIDS. Lou had been a graduate psychology student of mine, but he had had to drop out of school as his illness worsened. I had not seen him in months and had only spoken with him a few times on the phone. At that time, anyone with AIDS was dying very quickly.

One evening on the way to my meditation group, thoughts

of Lou kept running through my head, and I felt inspired to lead the others in a healing visualization. We mentally gathered together people we knew who were having health problems and visualized ourselves, and various spiritual masters, pouring energy into them. I imagined Lou in the center of the group being healed and then added a few other people I was aware of who were also in need of help. About a week later I received a call from Lou.

"Carolyn, did you do a healing on me last Tuesday at nine in the evening?" he began.

I had to think about it. Tuesday. That was my meditation night. And nine was about the time we had started the actual meditation. What had we been focusing on last Tuesday, I wondered. Oh, yes. We had offered healing energy to a number of people, and Lou had been one of my candidates.

"Yes, I guess I did." I replied. "How did you know?"

Lou said that last Tuesday night he had felt so ill that he had gone to bed very early, although he knew that he would not be able to sleep.

"Around nine I felt you come into my room and do a healing on me," Lou went on. "I knew it was you because I meditated with you that one time, and I know what your energy feels like. You did a healing on me, and then I fell into a deep sleep — I actually slept through the night for the first time in months. When I woke up in the morning, all my spots were gone! [He had Kaposi's Sarcoma, which mottles the skin.] I felt wonderful — better than I've felt in the last half year. My appetite came back, too, and I've put on fifteen pounds in the past week. I just had to call to thank you!"

Lou was no more surprised by this dramatic result than

I was. I believe that he was approaching a state of miracle-mindedness that night, and that the members of my group and I were miracle-minded. Either his guide, or my own, prompted me to make Lou an object of our prayers, encouraging him to set aside whatever negative thoughts had created his disease and were holding it in place. Once he made a miracle possible by becoming miracle-minded, the divine power available to him in his right mind did the rest.

However, I must also report that Lou's symptoms did eventually return, and that he died of AIDS about a year after this incident. It can, of course, be argued that it was merely a coincidence that Lou had a temporary remission he attributed to the spiritual energy he associated with me, at precisely the time I was — unbeknownst to him — praying for his healing. However, I'm convinced that Lou really did receive a miraculous healing, even if it did not produce a permanent cure.

Indeed, I suspect that the committee investigating miracles at Lourdes may be setting their standards a little too high in requiring the effect of miraculous healing to be permanent. As we shall see later in this book, an individual's present state of mind is the key to his or her experience. If someone whose conflicted thoughts were creating a deadly disease can be healed in an instant by shifting into a state of miracle-mindedness, a return to the old thoughts ought to be expected to reinstate the disease process.

Permanent healing depends upon permanent rejection of the thoughts and beliefs that caused the physical problem in the first place. But once someone leaves that peaceful altered state, he or she is at liberty to resume old ways of thinking. If the person does return to old thoughts, the disease might well return.

Besides, the fact that you successfully dodge an oncoming vehicle one day doesn't mean you'll never be run down by another. In the same way, I believe that if someone achieves a miraculous healing but eventually dies of the same disease, that doesn't mean she or he never really had a miracle in the first place.

THE BENEFITS OF PRAYING FOR OTHERS

I believe that the prayers of others, and especially of those who pray from a state of miracle-mindedness, encourage a troubled person to feel loved, to relax, and to withdraw from conflict into a peaceful state of miracle-mindedness. However, it is always the shift into peace and love that creates the miracle, and that perceptual shift is always up to the individual. One can successfully achieve miracle-mindedness without the prayers of others, and one can fail to achieve it with them.

Then too, being immersed in the loving prayers and good wishes of others may *improve* someone's mental state even when he or she doesn't achieve actual miracle-mindedness. That's probably why we see sick people who are prayed for healing somewhat faster, or surviving somewhat longer, than ones who aren't prayed for. To whatever extent the patient is able to let them in, the loving thoughts of others promote inner peace, and any degree of inner peace will facilitate healing and slow the course of disease. Perhaps that's why so many studies have found that terminally ill people who attend support groups, or have strong family or social ties, tend to live longer than those who don't.

I think this also explains the ability of deleterious thoughts to debilitate the mind, and consequently, the body of another. Whenever we think hostile thoughts about someone, it constitutes a psychic attack. Nevertheless, *people are impervious to suggestions with which they steadfastly refuse to agree*. We can ignore the blaming, belittling thoughts of others just as easily as we can ignore their healing ones. That's why voodoo and other forms of psychic attack can be so very dangerous to those who believe in them, while having little or no impact on those who don't.

But perhaps one of the best reasons to pray for others from a miracle-minded state is what it does for the one praying. That peaceful meditative state has been shown in the laboratory to benefit our bodies in a myriad of ways, by relieving stress, muscular tension, and pain; lowering blood pressure; reducing insulin resistance; boosting immune functioning; and more. Time spent in a peaceful, loving, and joyful state of consciousness is its own reward, and the present and future experiences our minds create for us on the basis of it produce abundance, love, and fulfillment. Further, since our thoughts are always available to other minds, our decision to be at peace uplifts and benefits everyone, and especially those we think about, or who think about us.

This concept of miracle-mindedness also adds to our understanding of why it is that so many people pray for miracles without receiving them. Recognizing that we can't solve a problem on our own and asking for divine help is an excellent beginning. But unless we take the additional step of entering miracle-mindedness, our divine guides are not in a position to correct our perceptions or act on our behalf. If we're unwittingly holding a problem in place by fearing illusions or harboring grievances, God and/or our guides would have to violate our free will in order to remove that problem, and that is something they will not do.

Things to Think About

1) Like those who experience miraculous escapes in connection with accidents and assaults, people who have spontaneous healings seek and find inner peace.

2) Have you ever noticed a wise and loving voice speaking to you in your mind? That's your divine guide.

3) As a Child of God, your mind is as powerful as that of every other person. No one can impose upon you unless you are willing to believe that you can be imposed upon.

Chapter Nine

Why Are Miracles So Rare?

Don't worry. Be happy.

— *Meher Baba*

Once we establish that miracles really are possible, the next question is, why are there so few individuals who actually experience them? I think there are four main reasons: we fail to recognize them, we aren't trained in creating them, sometimes we don't even want them, and sometimes we bury our troubled emotions and this gets in the way of them.

Front Page News

First, I think there may be many more instances of miracles than we ordinarily recognize. Because they fall outside the framework of our cultural thinking, miracles are not reported as such by mainstream news media. In the current intellectual climate, the mere fact that people claim to have experienced a miracle is often enough to make others write them off as cranks or religious fanatics. Under these conditions, it should not be surprising if folks don't always call public attention to their extraordinary experiences.

Such is the prejudice against miracles that even those to whom they occur may not identify them as such. For example, if a person diagnosed with an "incurable" illness recovers, everyone concerned may be much more likely to conclude that the initial diagnosis was wrong than to recognize that their prayers have been answered.

Then, too, because we ordinarily think of miracles as signs of special favor from God, even religious people often feel foolish and grandiose suggesting — or even believing — they've been the beneficiary of divine intervention. After all, they aren't Moses!

Another factor that accounts for the apparent rarity of miracles is that most folks hesitate to call something a *miracle* unless there is absolutely no other explanation for it. I am suggesting that evidence for miracles may be found in *improbable* events, as well as in *impossible* ones. If this is true, then many more of us have experienced supernatural phenomena or miracles than we realize. So, one answer to the question of why miracles appear to be so rare is that they may not really be rare at all — simply under-recognized and under-reported.

Accessing Miracles Is an Acquired Skill

It's also important to remember that many things exist as human potentials that are not realized in a given person. As a human being, I am theoretically capable of doing all the things that other humans can do, but in actuality I can only do the things that I personally have learned and am able to do. I cannot run a four-minute mile, set a broken leg, or even parallel park in under two minutes. But this is not evidence that such accomplishments are beyond the reach of everyone. And the fact that a given person is not aware of being able to access miracles is not evidence that miracles do not exist.

Notice that a lot of the people who told me their stories had had some spiritual training. They had invested time and effort in silencing their egos to turn within, and that may have made it much easier to enter a peaceful, miracle-minded state in an emergency, as well as more likely that they would try. Attaining the mental state necessary for miracles may simply be a skill that some people cultivate and others don't. If miracles become possible only when we enter a peaceful, loving altered state, they should not be expected by those who call upon God but refuse to release their disturbing perspective.

Miracles Are Not Always Welcome

As a psychologist, I'm aware that many troubled people do not truly want help, miraculous or otherwise. For example, a painful or disabling condition may unconsciously be regarded as less frightening than robust health if it elicits positive attention from others, provides monetary compensation, or releases the individual from onerous responsibilities he or she would otherwise be expected to meet. These unacknowledged, and sometimes even unconscious, reasons for putting up with an unsatisfying state of affairs are what psychologists call "secondary gain." I may not like the back pain, but I may love the workers' compensation benefits and the fact that no one expects me to resume my lousy job.

Also, I suspect we sometimes put ourselves in difficult situations because we are trying to compel ourselves to learn something. A divorced woman floundering around financially may be creating an opportunity to master self-reliance or to learn to quit behaving like a martyr and assert her legal rights more effectively. All of us can look back upon periods of our lives that were pure hell at the time, but which we now realize taught us important lessons.

It is my belief that all illnesses and other misfortunes are caused by misthought at the level of the ego. We'll discuss this more in chapter 12, but here it is enough to say that the ego thinks in opposition to God. God wants us to be happy, but our happiness is not high on our ego's list of priorities. There are always reasons why we suffer, but never *good* reasons.

Miracles may not even be welcome if a person does not want to believe in them. This becomes a self-fulfilling prophecy. If we believe we can't be helped — or at least not in this way, or by this person — that's what our experience will verify. Even a true miracle worker cannot overcome a given individual's resistance to miracles.

For example, the New Testament tells us that Jesus was unable to perform many miracles when he revisited the town where he had grown up. ("A prophet is not without honor, save in his own country, and in his own house"; Matthew 13:53–57.) His old acquaintances evidently thought it beneath them to accept help from the little boy who used to run around their village. Their resistance to the idea that Jesus might know something they didn't made it impossible for him to play a role in their healing.

If you are intent upon believing that miracles are unreal or fraudulent, then you will not experience them purely because *you prefer not to.* The decision you've made is that you prefer your skepticism to having your problem solved in a way that would force you to release it. God and all agents of the divine respect your free will and do not remove problems you want to keep or that you want to solve by yourself. It is your mind that has created the problem, and it isn't going to go away without your consent.

For miracles to occur, it isn't necessary that you have unwavering faith in God or a would-be miracle worker, although that seems to help. But you must be at least open to the possibility of healing and genuinely willing to see your problem disappear.

Many physicians would agree that all healing depends upon the patient's inner decision to release the problem to solution. A medication that heals one person may be ineffective for another, while a third is allergic to it, and a fourth gets well without treatment. Our unconscious ambivalence may interfere with our ability to accept miracles in precisely the same way that it limits our response to the healing efforts of medical practitioners.

BURIED THOUGHTS BECOME BARRIERS

When we exclude thoughts from consciousness through psychological defenses like denial, projection, and repression, it is as if we assign subordinate parts of our personality to 1) act on those thoughts, and at the same time 2) make sure they stay hidden from consciousness.

"Jenkins, get this memory [thought, impulse, whatever] out of here and don't let it back into awareness under any circumstances! And then also get rid of the memory that we ever had this conversation. I was never here. We never spoke about this. Got that? It never happened."

"What never happened, sir?"

"Excellent, Jenkins! Keep up the good work!"

Of course, all of this is nothing more than a game we play with ourselves. Disowned thoughts only remain unavailable to awareness as long as we wish to keep them that way. Conscious or unconscious, my mind is, after all, my mind. It has no option but to do my bidding. If I ever really want to recover that memory, and won't take "no" for an answer, the underling will have to produce it.

"Jenkins, let me have that extremely embarrassing impulse I gave you to forget."

"What impulse, sir? I don't remember you giving me anything to forget."

"Knock it off, Jenkins. You know the impulse I mean. Get it out here, now!"

"Are you sure you...?"

"Yes, dammit! Cough it up!"

"Right away, sir."

So what good are psychological defenses that hide unacceptable thoughts from conscious awareness if they can't make them permanently disappear from our minds? Their purpose is ultimately to provide plausible deniability. That way we can present a semblance of honesty and sincerity when we are being anything but! And the best part is that we ourselves are the only ones who need to be convinced that what we're saying is true.

"I beg your pardon! You say I did what? I'm afraid you're quite mistaken. If I'd done something like that I'd certainly remember it. Well, since you insist, let me just check again.

"Jenkins, this lady claims we have an attitude of hostility toward women stored away somewhere. Do we have anything like that on file?"

"Oh, no sir. I'm familiar with everything we have, and I assure you, there's nothing like that!"

"Very good, Jenkins. Well, I hope that satisfies you, madam. As you can see, we have no record of any such thing ever occurring. Now if you'll excuse me, I'm a very busy man.

"Can you believe the nerve of that woman, Jenkins?! How dare she suggest that I would ever behave in a hostile manner toward a woman?!"

"Disgraceful! She's probably quite insane. It's a shame you were troubled, sir."

The best liars, you see, are those who manage to believe their own lies. They exude an aura of certainty, innocence, and rectitude that genuinely honest people can't match, because genuinely honest people tend to be troubled by nagging doubts about what their unconscious minds may have been up to without their conscious knowledge. Needless to say, these sorts of repressed emotions and thoughts can block miracle-mindedness, as I once found out for myself.

CAROLYN: LOOKING FOR SYMPATHY

Some years ago I had a fall and injured my right shoulder. It was so painful to lift my arm away from my body that I began restricting my range of motion to let it heal. But instead of healing, the pain only got worse. Months later my right arm had become practically useless. It was by then much weaker than my left, despite the fact that I am right-handed. I experienced sickening pain every time I moved it the wrong way.

What did my doctor say about it? The truth is, it never seriously occurred to me to see a doctor. I just kept expecting my shoulder to heal on its own.

I only consulted an orthopedist after an incident where an unplanned movement caused such nauseating pain that I could only stop in my tracks panting in agony. When my husband — a man I ordinarily adore — said, "What's wrong?" I turned on him in fury and lambasted him for not even remembering that I had an injured shoulder and arm. I told the bewildered man that if he had cared anything about me, he'd have seen that I got medical attention months ago. Even as I was saying it, it was obvious to me that as an adult, and the one in the best position to know how serious the problem was, it was surely up to me to call a doctor. Nevertheless, I was behaving as though the whole thing was my husband's fault.

I finally did see a doctor, a rotator cuff injury was diagnosed, and I started physical therapy to regain the use of my right arm. I worked hard on stretching exercises at home, and I was making good progress, although my range of motion had become so severely limited that my physical therapist warned me it might never get all the way back to normal.

A week or two into therapy, with my arm somewhat more mobile and less painful but a long way from being well, I went out of town on a business trip. With nothing much to do in my motel room one evening, I meditated and asked Jesus to heal my shoulder. Then I heard him say, "Do you really want a miracle?"

"Yes!" I responded. "That would be so cool!"

"Are you ready to look at the reason you did this to yourself?" he continued.

"Sure," I replied hesitantly. "But I don't know what I did, or why. Can you help me out?"

Jesus then explained that I had kept my shoulder from healing as a means of getting attention from my husband. To my very great embarrassment, my guide told me that I had entertained the idea that if there were something physically wrong with me, Arnie would become even more concerned and nurturing. Since a sneaky idea like this would not stand up very long in the light of consciousness, I had consigned it to my unconscious mind. Once there, it created problems with my shoulder and arm that I thought would be guaranteed to worry my husband and reap for me a rich harvest of sympathetic attention.

In this, Jesus went on, I had completely misread the situation, since Arnie saw me as a strong, capable person and invariably forgot about my shoulder the minute I stopped talking about it. Given that this ploy of mine was such a dismal failure, Jesus remarked, I might want to just cut my losses and stop portraying myself as injured and suffering.

This account of my problem jibed all-too-well with my furious reaction to Arnie. Clearly I had been waiting for months for him to pity my suffering and take the initiative with respect to my healing. That emotional explosion was the sound of me getting it that it wasn't going to happen.

While I couldn't help feeling a bit disgruntled at Jesus's unflattering account of my behavior, I knew he was right.

"Okay," I acknowledged, "it was a stupid, mean-spirited thing to do, and I guess I owe Arnie an apology. Now can we heal the arm?"

"Sure," he replied. "All that's actually wrong with it at this point is that the muscles, nerves, and connective tissue have tightened up from lack of use. You just need to instruct them to relax and then stretch them until they allow normal movement."

I sat down on the floor and braced my arm against the bed and began stretching. It was excruciating!

"It feels like my arm is about to snap right off," I complained. "Isn't there some way to make it not hurt so much?"

"Your nerves are reporting pain when nothing is really wrong because that's what you've instructed them to do. They're *your* nerves, and they do what *you* say. You need to instruct them to relax — assure them that the stretching is perfectly safe. Send them love, and visualize them loosening. Tell them that you are revoking the instructions you gave them before, and that they no longer have to prevent motion to protect you."

I did my best, and in a few hours I had stretched my arm to the point where I recovered a normal range of motion. The nauseating pain was now only the dull ache of overexerted muscles. Even that was gone by morning.

When I told Arnie about all of this and tendered the

apology due him, he was very surprised to hear me talk about the amount of pain and disability I'd had. What we finally realized is that in his family, people complain loud and long about any little ache or pain. As a result, Arnie had learned to tune out most of what he heard. The people in my family are fairly stoical, and my occasional allusion to my shoulder barely registered on his radar.

"Next time," he advised, "try rolling around on the floor and gnashing your teeth. I'm pretty sure that would make an impression on me."

Miracles Are an Inside Job

Now, you may be wondering in what sense this was a miracle, since I had to do all the work myself. I consider it the restoration of normal function in an arm that had been practically useless a few hours earlier. My physical therapist was not optimistic about complete healing, and I'm sure he would not have believed it could occur in a few hours. Then, too, the inner guide I believe to be Jesus called it a "miracle," and he ought to know. In *A Course in Miracles*, a miracle is defined as a shift into right-mindedness, which certainly did occur here.

The main point to remember is that miracles are inevitably an inside job. The recipient of the miracle *always* has to change his or her mind in order to reverse a bad situation. Even when it appears that a miraculous healing has been performed by a supernatural being, a faith healer, the prayers of others, or one's own prayers at a special holy place, I don't believe healing would have occurred unless the recipient was miracle-minded, which is to say, willing to give up both the symptoms and the misguided goals that led to them. This is why so many attempts to heal seem to fail. Free will guarantees that no one can go around curing people who still have a use for their symptoms, or who are not willing to recognize and change the mistaken beliefs that hold them in place.

What a miracle worker *can* do is believe in the possibility of healing and help the sufferer focus on the real problem — the person's limiting thoughts and beliefs. It doesn't matter whether she or he is present with us when we need healing or praying for us at a distance, since mind is not limited by the body. Loving intentions can be communicated telepathically, in much the same way that someone can comfort or encourage us, or suggest a different way of thinking about our problem over the telephone. The suggestion doesn't compel us to do anything, but if we are open to it, it may prompt us to make a needed revision in our own thinking.

Does Healing Depend on Full Self-Awareness?

I don't believe it is necessary to be completely aware of all our unconscious motives before we can experience healing — as long as we are truly ready to give up the secondary gain that we once thought worth the pain. For example, if a woman who is financially dependent upon compensation for her disability suddenly wins the lottery, her symptoms may quickly disappear, since they no longer serve any useful purpose. But she may never even notice the relationship between the windfall and her healing.

Once your ego's unconscious goal in maintaining suffering

is given up, with or without your conscious knowledge, you are free to resolve the painful condition in whatever way is most acceptable to you. For some people this may involve an instantaneous healing they believe to be miraculous. For others it may take the form of a gradual process of improvement they attribute to good medical care, acupuncture, herbal remedies, careful diet, or to any other healing modality in which the individual is prepared to believe.

Take my story above. I had been unconsciously instructing my shoulder and arm to tighten up and remain immobile. I'd also told the nerves to report excruciating pain in connection with movement, even though the movement posed no real danger.

At the point at which I yelled at Arnie, I think I had gotten it that this shoulder problem wasn't working out the way I had hoped it would. I didn't consciously recognize my reasons for creating and maintaining the symptom, but I was aware of feeling deeply disappointed with the whole enterprise and just wanting to be done with the pain and disability. That was the point at which I sought healing from a physician, a physical therapist, and, ultimately, from Jesus. I believe that since I was ready to give up the symptom, healing could have come in any form I was prepared to accept. Jesus's advice simply encouraged me to realize there was no good reason not to get it over with quickly.

When you are seeking healing, it is always a good idea to affirm your willingness to give up any and all motives — whether conscious or unconscious — that might be holding the problem in place. This authorizes the unconscious — your personal "Jenkins" — to release hidden problematic thoughts or to kick them back up into conscious awareness for reassessment. Take, for example, this healing affirmation recommended by an entity called Rajpur, who is channeled by Paul Tuttle at the Northwest Foundation for *A Course in Miracles*:

> It is the intent of my body to express my individuality perfectly. I authorize my body to release anything that is not necessary to its perfect functioning. And I hereby revoke any prior — conscious or unconscious — authorizations to the contrary.[1]

I was interested to come upon what seems like an ancient version of this affirmation found in the library of the Assyrian king Ashurbanipal (668–633 BCE).[2]

> May the god whom I either know or do not know be at peace with me. May the goddess whom I either know or do not know be at peace with me.

If you believe that your affliction is caused by the ill will of a god or goddess rather than by the fact that you misguidedly authorized "Jenkins" to act against your true best interests, this is precisely how you might address the problem.

In other words, there are times when we can give up the unconscious need for a painful condition without ever realizing we *had* such a need. However, as long as the motive underlying a problem continues in full force, the symptom will either resist healing or take some other form (a process psychoanalysts call *symptom substitution*). As long as you fail to recognize and reject destructive motives, there is a danger that your unconscious mind will go ahead and act upon them, arranging circumstances that your conscious mind finds disturbing.

Accepting the Implications of Miracles

Even if we are genuinely prepared to relinquish a painful condition, it does not follow that we are prepared to accept *miraculous* help. The whole idea of miracles is disturbing to a lot of people — probably because it implies the existence of God, whom many regard as a vengeful punisher of sin. I suspect that fear of divine retribution makes some people shy away from the idea of God altogether, and this may make nonmiraculous help far more acceptable than the miraculous kind. In a culture where evidence of a supernatural power may be deeply frightening, it should not be surprising if most healings are attributed to traditional medicine, and if most dangers unexpectedly averted at the last minute are written off as "luck."

I think, too, that some religious people actually believe that suffering in this world will reduce their penance in the next. They imagine that when God sees how miserable they have been throughout their lives, He will be moved to pity them and let them off with only a little punishment in the afterlife. People who believe this would be unwilling to give up their suffering because they believe it protects them from a much worse fate.

This is where psychotherapy comes in; indeed, as we've seen, miracles and self-awareness go hand in hand. No one consciously desires illness, financial problems, personal rejection, or other forms of misery. Nevertheless, we may have ill-considered beliefs and mental habits that create such experiences, as well as hidden reasons for thinking that we need or deserve them. Good transpersonal, insight-oriented psychotherapy can help people understand and reverse self-defeating mental behavior and open them up to healing in all areas of their lives.

Things to Think About

1) Free will means that people must be willing to change to solve their self-created problems. This ordinarily requires that the unconscious reasons or needs for the problems be made conscious.

2) If you're hoping for a miracle, begin by exploring your innermost thoughts about your problem. In what ways would your life be more difficult or less secure if the problem were removed? Do you secretly feel you deserve the problem or derive some benefit from it?

Chapter Ten

Groping the Cosmic Elephant

Form, as matter, is an illusion. Form, as Spirit,
held together with the Intent to express a divine idea, is Truth.
The misunderstanding comes when it is not perceived that all
form is an idea — an idea which
has substance, an idea which has visibility to the
infinite Mind of which it is the Creation.

— Rajpur

There is a well-known Sufi parable about four blind men who are introduced to an elephant for the first time. They approach the enormous animal with lively curiosity and grope whatever part of it they can reach.

"Oh," says the first, attempting to encircle a huge leg with his arms, "I understand now. An elephant is very much like a tree."

"No," the second corrects him while reaching up to feel the vast expanse of the elephant's side. "An elephant is very much like a wall."

"You are both mistaken," declares the third as he tries to hang onto the great beast's probing trunk. "An elephant is very much like a snake."

"I cannot imagine where you get such ideas!" exclaims the fourth, holding up the tail. "It is perfectly obvious that an elephant is just like a rope!"

This story has often been used to illustrate the discrepancies between the findings of scientists and mystics. It underscores the fact that empirical observations are always made from some limited theoretical perspective and focused upon a narrowly restricted field of study. The conclusions arrived at by this method may all be correct enough as far as they go, but they may nevertheless fail to capture the essence of the entire phenomenon.

Through intuition (literally, "inner teaching," which implies the presence of an inner teacher or guide), some mystics seem to be able to catch a glimpse of the cosmic "elephant" as an integrated being engaged in purposeful activities. Scientists, on the other hand, have necessarily tried to get it to hold still for a minute, so that they could meticulously analyze a handy patch of trunk, leg, torso, or tail in hopes of piecing together the whole from the sum of its parts. Small wonder that they sometimes do not seem to be talking about the same thing!

However, the Sufi parable also suggests that if the blind men were to continue exploring the elephant long enough — sharing information with each other along the way — they would eventually derive a more integrated understanding of their subject. When their observations had encompassed the entire living entity and its habitual activities, you would expect that their descriptions would begin to sound very much like those of a sighted person.

And this is precisely what has happened to physicists. They have finally gathered enough information about the universe to realize that, taken as a whole, it is actually very much the way certain mystics have described it. Relativity and quantum theory have opened a window on a mysterious and arguably "supernatural" dimension of reality. As physicist Fritjof Capra[1] and others have pointed out, these days it is sometimes difficult to tell the difference between the statements of modern physicists and certain teachings of ancient spiritual masters. Let's see what light contemporary physics has to shed upon our investigation of miracles.

THE EXISTENCE OF MIND

By the middle of the twentieth century, a "consciousness revolution" was gaining strength within physics and spilling over into other disciplines. The theory that science could dispense with mental constructs like *thoughts* and *ideas* was simply no longer tenable.

For one thing, the role of an observing consciousness is central to relativity theory. At the quantum level, physical things cannot even be known to exist until they are observed. Science writer Norman Friedman explains:

> The paradox is this: we need particles of matter to make up the objects of our everyday world (including us), and we need an object in that very everyday world (us) to define and observe those particles. Observation implies consciousness. Any construct that purports to describe reality in terms of contemporary physics clearly must include a role for consciousness.[2]

Today the majority of scientists in all fields accept the idea that mental phenomena are real. Indeed, nowadays there is serious question about whether *physical* things really exist as anything more than temporary aggregations of energy that assume one form for a while and then flow into another. Many scientists believe that the universe may fundamentally be one of mind rather than matter. As the distinguished British astronomer Sir James Jeans put it: "The stream of knowledge is heading toward a non-mechanical reality; the universe begins to look more like a great thought than like a great machine."[3]

Further, it has become apparent that this "great thought" is not subject to the natural laws that regulate the activity of matter within the physical world. For example, quantum theory implies that when two particles interact and then separate, they continue to influence each other instantaneously — which is to say, faster than the speed of light. In the 1960s, physicist and mathematician John Stewart Bell came up with a thought experiment to verify this prediction, and when advances in instrumentation finally made it possible to actually perform the experiment, the prediction was found to be true.

Since it is known that nothing in our three-dimensional universe *can* exceed the speed of light, physicists concluded that there must be some "deeper" level of our universe where quantum particles are instantaneously connected — *an invisible, causal dimension that exists outside the natural world and is not subject to the constraints of space and time!* And what else would the supernatural realm be?

The "Deeper" Level of the Universe

Physicist David Bohm proposed that the physical world comes into existence when minds interact with what he called "hierarchies of implicate informational structures."[4]

Within this conceptual "implicate order," Bohm hypothesized that all possible futures are "enfolded" as potential. He believed that when a particular idea becomes the focus of someone's attention, it is conceptually "unfolded" and brought into physical form as a set of circumstances that symbolically embodies that idea.

This is to say that a thought in someone's mind is actually "made manifest" through the interest of that individual in having the corresponding experience. As Norman Friedman puts it: "The observer thus becomes a creator and gives the system its form. Without the observer, the system is in a state of potential, waiting to come into existence."[5]

Certain mystical traditions have long maintained that thoughts are made manifest in the physical world through the concentrated attention and belief of those who think them. As Serge King, a Hawaiian spiritual teacher or "Kahuna" explains, this concept is at the very core of Hawaiian mysticism.

> The most fundamental idea in Huna philosophy is that we each create our own personal experience of reality, by our beliefs, interpretations, actions and reactions, thoughts and feelings. It is not that our reality is created for us as a result of these personal expressions, but that we are creators, co-creators with the Universe itself. Huna is all about learning to do that consciously. This idea, however, is not unique to Huna. It is shared, though often only in the esoteric teachings, by virtually every religion known to man. Sadly, it is seldom widely taught or practiced.[6]

This means that each person's experience of the world is actually an illusion generated within his or her own mind. It also implies that each such personal illusion is unique. *Your* world will appear to you any way *you* believe it to be. And if our thoughts *create* the illusory physical world we seem to see around us on a moment-to-moment basis, it follows that changing our thoughts should *change* the world we experience. Is it possible that in studying the way the physical world is brought into existence by the activity of the mind, scientists have been quietly elucidating the mechanism by which sudden changes in one's mental state produce sudden changes in one's physical circumstances that have no apparent physical cause? Could this be how miracles are created?

Remember how in many of the stories so far, people faced danger with what appeared to be an irrational conviction that everything was going to work out fine? I suspect that this "faith" in their continued well-being may have played a vital role in selecting which one of a number of possible futures they would go on to actualize. Here is another such story to consider.

HEIDI: WIGGLING A TOE

Heidi was a San Diego teenager I encountered on the same talk show where I met Christine and Dr. Scott. A couple of years earlier, she had broken her back in an automobile accident. She was cut out of the wreckage paralyzed from the waist down, and it was greatly feared that she would remain that way for the rest of her life. Many people close to her, including some of her doctors, believe that Heidi's recovery from this serious spinal cord displacement was miraculous.

Heidi's neurosurgeon described her injury as the worst he'd ever seen of its kind. On a scale of 1 to 5, her doctors estimated her chances of ever being able to walk again as "0 to

1." Although they did not want to be discouraging, they admitted when pressed that they had never seen anyone come back from such a severe spinal cord displacement. As one of her physicians privately confided to Heidi's rehabilitation nurse, "That's one kid who will never walk again!"

Heidi told me that her constant prayer throughout her ordeal was "Lord, just get me through this. You can let me die, or you can let me walk away, or you can help me accept what will happen. But just get me through this somehow."

Notice that, like many others who received miracles, Heidi asked for divine help but did not presume to tell God specifically what the outcome should be. As she saw it, if it was God's will that she die, or that she survive as a paraplegic, she was prepared to accept her situation and try to make the best of it. It seemed to her that with God's support, she could somehow be all right no matter what happened to her. Her focus was upon maintaining a sense of inner peace, whatever occurred.

Nevertheless, Heidi believed in miracles, and she never let go of the hope that she would walk again. Whenever her doctors and nurses commented on her poor prognosis, Heidi's response was always, "Never tell me that!" She knew her chances were slim, but she was determined to do everything in her power to make a complete recovery. Like others who experienced deliverance, Heidi denied the *inevitability* of a negative outcome, although she did not deny its *possibility*.

Heidi said that as her days in the hospital wore on with no evidence of improvement, it was increasingly difficult to keep her hopes alive. Finally, in desperation, she prayed, "Lord, just give me something — some small sign of progress that I can work to improve on." The next day, she discovered that she was able to wiggle a toe ever so slightly. As far as Heidi was concerned, it was the sign from God for which she had been praying. She set to work with all her concentration, focusing upon this little movement and working to expand it. By concentrating totally on the one encouraging sign she had been given, I believe that Heidi focused the power of her mind to actualize a very improbable, but nonetheless possible, future.

Contrary to everyone's predictions, Heidi walked out of the hospital one month after her accident. When I met her, she was walking almost normally — a slight limp was all that remained of her former paraplegia. She is convinced that her recovery was a gift from God, but I want to emphasize that it was also one she had a hand in cocreating. By relentlessly maintaining the necessary mental focus, she seems to have found a way to bring something that was only a distant possibility into physical manifestation as her "reality."

Was this an actual miracle — an instance where a supernatural power interfered with nature? Or is it better understood as an extreme example of the principles by which everything in the natural world is brought into manifestation? We'll take up this question in the next chapter.

Things to Think About

1) If the things you think about tend to manifest as your personal experience, what have you been thinking?

2) Your thoughts should be constantly for the highest and best outcome.

Chapter Eleven

Believing Is Seeing

A Son of God can recognize his power
in one instant and change the world in the next.
That is because, by changing his mind,
he has changed the most powerful device
that was ever given him for change.

— *A Course in Miracles*

*T*he dynamic African-American preacher Dr. Frederick
Eikerenkoetter — affectionately known as Reverend
Ike — used to say that each of us "purchases" experiences in
this world by "paying" attention to them. Since every person
has an equal capacity for taking an interest in things, we all
have equal power to actualize our will. What makes the difference in our fortunes is *what* we elect to pay attention *to*.
We quite literally "buy into" whatever experiences we allow
to capture our attention.

Thus, when we "invest" attention and belief in the possibility that circumstance "X" will occur, our minds actually
begin to bring X into manifestation in our physical experience.

The more time and energy we devote to anticipating X, the more likely it becomes that we will experience it. For example, the fact that we are worrying about being poor and lonely constitutes a choice on our part to dwell upon those conditions mentally. Seeing our interest in loneliness and want, our unconscious minds respond by "unfolding" further experiences of poverty and social isolation in our physical experience. "Jenkins" strikes again!

This means that our decisions about what to think about and believe exert a profound influence over the things that happen in our lives. For instance, consider the saying, "I've often been broke, but I've never been poor." Both "poor" and "broke" describe a state where one's financial resources are inadequate to meet one's needs, but "broke" is the term likely to be used by someone who regards himself as *temporarily* financially embarrassed, while "poor" would be the word chosen by one who has little hope that things are ever going to improve. And because these differing interpretations influence what happens next, someone who sees himself as "broke" is a lot more likely to turn the situation around than one who regards himself as "poor."

MAKING REALITY

The universe appears to function in such a way that whatever we believe is true is illustrated by our subsequent experience. Our minds manifest the conditions we expect to find. And it's important to notice that this process is completely counterintuitive. We ordinarily assume that "seeing is believing," which is to say that we think we believe certain things because we've seen the evidence that that's the way things really are. What the supernatural perspective I'm presenting here suggests is just the opposite: "Believing is seeing."

This means that you have a free choice about what to believe about yourself, the world, and other people. But since your beliefs actually *cause* the kinds of things you expect to manifest, your future experiences will always seem to verify those expectations. If a woman embraces the belief that "men are no damn good," she has set a course for a very disappointing love life. If a man constantly affirms, "I love women and women love me," witness how much better his romantic luck will be.

Now if only one person is affected by belief in X, then it is largely up to that individual whether or not to believe X into manifestation in his or her experience. For example, because Heidi's disability directly affected only herself, she was probably in complete control of the outcome. The prayers and positive thoughts of her loved ones undoubtedly encouraged her to keep her hopes high and strive to maintain a state of miracle-mindedness. But ultimately it was up to her what possibility to believe in, and so actualize. Had she lost hope, or given way to self-pity, her negative thoughts would have generated negative outcomes instead of the very positive one she ultimately achieved.

Heidi's situation illustrates the advantage that people who believe in miracles have in desperate situations. Since they are not limited by consideration of what seems most likely to happen, or what other people consider possible, they are free to go on hoping for the best in the face of overwhelming evidence to the contrary. And since their expectations and beliefs influence subsequent events in the physical world, this so-called irrational hope often pays off. As we've seen, the decision to believe that desperate situations can turn out well is highly characteristic of people who go on to achieve miracles. If it's all a matter of self-fulfilling prophecies, it makes sense to predict the outcome you'd truly like to have.

But what if a situation involves the fates of many people? For example, what if X represents "world peace"? Changing collective illusions requires collective action. By remaining at peace ourselves, and expecting, visualizing, and working for world peace, we increase the likelihood that it will occur. However, everyone else contributes a vote as well. As long as the majority of people on earth believe international conflicts are inevitable, that "some people will just never learn," or that they personally have something to gain through uncooperative or aggressive behavior, wars will continue. What actually manifests at any given time is something like the sum of everyone's positive and negative expectations about that situation. As is said in *Conversations with God*, FATE can be seen as an acronym for "From All Thoughts Everywhere."[1]

Nevertheless, whatever actual situation manifests, most individuals are going to *perceive* it according to their own preconceptions. Imagine, for example, a group of political commentators listening to a candidate's speech. Depending upon their party affiliations, each ignores or downplays some aspects of what's been said, exaggerates others, and generally gives his or her own personal spin to the rest. Hearing them speak about it later, you might not even realize they all heard the same speech. Until we awaken spiritually, we constantly distort our perceptions so as to uncover "proof" we were right all along in whatever we chose to believe.

Where do we get these preconceptions? Most of us allow our beliefs, expectations, and perceptions to be molded by family, culture, religion, and education. By constantly thinking and reacting as we have been taught and conditioned, we continually access the same sorts of outcomes from the infinite possibilities available. In this manner, we produce for ourselves the experience of a stable, predictable world, although not necessarily a rewarding one. This accounts for both the continuity we ordinarily experience as well as the "miraculous" discontinuity that is possible when we radically change our thinking.

As a result of our insistence upon seeing everything from our own unique point of view, what is realistic in one person's private illusion may have been ruled out of the question in another's. For example, I will never forget a woman named Nancy, with whom I used to work, who expressed wistful envy over my account of an enjoyable trip to a distant city.

"You have some vacation time coming," I reminded her. "Why don't you go there yourself?"

"Oh!" Nancy replied in a shocked tone. "I couldn't do that! If I left town, everyone would think I had gone away to have an abortion!"

The idea that anyone would make such a bizarre association would simply never have crossed my mind, but this woman was living in her own private world where "everyone" would leap at an opportunity to judge and condemn her. That was one scary little world she had going, and I was glad that I was not obliged to live there myself!

WORRY IS THE ENEMY

Once we realize that simply thinking about a particular circumstance makes it more likely to occur in our experience, it becomes clear that worrying about something tends to *attract* it. Whenever we worry, we are using the creative power of our minds to generate the very circumstances we least want to have happen. But that isn't all. In fearing something or someone, we simultaneously *grant it the power to hurt us*.

Since our beliefs and expectations select the future we'll experience, we can unwittingly *give permission* for something bad to happen to us, just by choosing to perceive the situation as one that justifies fear. Remember, without realizing it, each of us is writing our own life script. If I create a character and attribute to him the power to injure me, my story may take a turn I'd rather it didn't. On the other hand, if I treat everyone as a friend, I am affirming my belief that they will not harm me and energizing that possibility.

As we've seen in the many stories of deliverance people have shared with me, maintaining a peaceful, fearless state of mind is essential to one's safety. What follows is another striking example of how an endangered individual seems to have derailed an attack by declining the fearful/angry victim role a would-be assailant was trying to thrust upon her.

Dona: Twelve Feet Tall

In her early twenties, Dona once noticed a well-dressed man she later described as "built like a football player" entering a grocery store she was leaving. She was dimly aware that he had given her a glance as they passed. Continuing on her way without a second thought, Dona walked several blocks to the laundry building behind her Los Angeles apartment house and went inside to begin her wash. When she heard the garden gate creak, she looked out the window and discovered with a sinking feeling that the man she had seen in the market had followed her home.

Before Dona could get to the only door, the stranger planted himself in it, blocking her exit. Dona described him as "obviously working himself up" for some sort of action. He was flushed and breathing hard, and his nostrils were flaring. She felt that he was watching her gloatingly, the way a cat watches a mouse before pouncing on it.

Dona remembered then that there had been a series of rapes in her neighborhood and saw that this man fit the sketches and descriptions published in the papers. It dawned on her that she was cornered in this isolated building by the so-called Mid-Wilshire Rapist.

With this realization came a momentary sense of panic that reminded her of the way she had felt as a child when she was being beaten by her stepfather. This memory was followed by a surge of determination never again to be anyone's victim.

"I just thought, 'I'll be damned if I'll let any man terrorize me!'"

Suddenly, Dona found herself becoming oddly peaceful and self-confident. She coolly met the man's gloating gaze, and it was her impression that a psychic message passed between them through their eyes.

"His eyes invited me to recognize his power over me and be afraid. I calmly but firmly sent him the psychic message back, 'This isn't for me. You've got the wrong person.'

"It was like being in an altered state," Dona continued. "I felt that our minds were communicating with each other. The man was trying to persuade me to enter a state of consciousness that would be complementary to his so that we could act out a drama together. He would be the powerful aggressor, and I would be the terrified victim. All he needed in order to attack me was for me to get scared. He was waiting to see that I was afraid — that's what rape victims are supposed to do. And I saw that he could not carry out his plan if I refused to match energy with him. I just flatly refused his invitation to go into fear, or to credit him with the power to hurt me. And I could see that it really confused him."

Having declined the "invitation," Dona experienced herself becoming enormously large and powerful. "This guy was over six feet tall and easily twice my weight, but in my mind I suddenly began to feel as though I was twelve feet tall, and he was just some puny little creature that couldn't possibly imagine itself strong enough to interfere with me.

"I knew that I had to get out of there, so I just locked onto his mind with this sense of being enormous and powerful, and I walked straight at him where he was blocking the door. He looked surprised when I just kept coming, but at the last minute he backed out of my way and let me pass. As I went by him, I saw him hold up his hands defensively, the way people do when they are trying to ward off something powerful and dangerous. I know that in his mind, too, I was big and strong while he was little and weak."

Dona walked to her apartment and locked herself in. The man made no attempt to follow her. "It sounds crazy, but I know that I kept him from attacking me by not matching his expectations of how I was supposed to behave. If he had detected any fear in my mind, he would have been on me in a second."

Dona learned from the newspapers that the Mid-Wilshire Rapist went on to murder his next victim. She is uncomfortably aware of how close she came to being that next victim.

Establishing Consensus

Every interpersonal situation is both an improvisation and a collaboration. The particular experiences two people come together to act out must be selected by both from among the many futures possible for each. Doing this requires mutually agreed-upon definitions. If their definitions and interpretations are completely incompatible, it's hard for either to know what to do.

When Dona simply refused to accept the victim role her would-be assailant was pressing her to enact, it became difficult — if not actually impossible — for him to proceed as planned. How is a rapist to satisfy his lust for conquest with a woman who is neither frightened nor angry? How is he supposed to physically overpower one who insists upon casting herself as twelve feet tall and enormously powerful?

"But she wasn't *really* twelve feet tall," you may protest. The point is that there is nothing "real" going on within personal illusions. Here, all that existed were two minds that couldn't agree about their respective sizes and abilities. The would-be rapist contended he was big enough to overpower and rape Dona. She contended he was not. Her lack of cooperation effectively blocked him from "unfolding" and acting out the scenario he had in mind — at least with her.

Unfortunately, most of us are all too willing to allow a determined person to define the nature of an interaction. Well-socialized individuals automatically assume complementary roles to smooth their interactions with others, and when someone powerful and aggressive comes along and threatens them, they're prone to cooperate by slipping into the victim role. In so doing, they actually give their would-be assailant an opportunity to victimize them through their willingness to join the assailant in dreaming that that is what happens.

We can now see that some surprising beneficial reversals of fortune may come down to the ability of a miracle-minded individual to abandon an angry or fearful interpretation of events that was causing a disturbing possible future to "unfold" in her or his experience. Instead of continuing to see a would-be assailant as a dangerous enemy, the miracle worker redefines him, perhaps as a confused and frightened friend or as someone harmless. If she is steadfast in insisting upon this new perspective, the other person may feel obliged to change his own script to reestablish some basis for the relationship. Of course, if the other party doesn't want to give up his plan, he's free to look elsewhere for a partner more willing to adopt a role that complements the one he wishes to play.

THE LIMITATIONS OF MANIFESTATION

This mechanism by which our consciousness generates our physical illusion is the basis for the positive-thinking movement. Adherents urge others to think only positive thoughts and to shift their negative beliefs by repeatedly affirming and visualizing the state of affairs they desire.

However, it's not quite as simple as it is sometimes made to sound. For one thing, there are limits to any individual's powers of manifestation.

One of them relates to the abilities of others to manifest what *they* think. Within the consensual illusion we all share, everyone competes to fulfill their desires, and no one person can expect to win all the marbles. Thus, disciplined concentration upon your goals can help you achieve the *kinds* of experiences you want to have, but not necessarily every specific thing you desire.

Let's say, for example, that you dream of being the pope. This is a field of endeavor where there are seldom more than two or three job openings within anyone's lifetime, and a great many well-qualified individuals aspire to the same position. Nevertheless, while you may not be among the lucky few to be named Supreme Pontiff, that doesn't mean you couldn't manifest the experience of being an influential spiritual leader.

Similarly, while we can't all marry Antonio Banderas or Angelina Jolie, we can aspire to find a life partner who embodies the qualities we admire in them. Positive thinking on your part isn't going to allow you to violate the free will of anyone else. You can't compel some particular person to love you, but you can attract a particular kind of mate.

But perhaps the most serious problem with using manifestation techniques consciously is that unless you are using them from a state of miracle-mindedness, *you* aren't really using them at all — your ego is. The ego is a false sense of self, grounded in misperceptions about our real identity. The problem is that as long as you identify with your ego, you are lending it your God-given creative power so that it can achieve *its* goals. And since the things your ego wants will never satisfy *you*, you're likely to spend your life seeking wealth, status, admiration, power, material possessions, and relationships that look good on the outside but provide no real love or joy. No matter how many of your ego's goals you fulfill, you'll wind up feeling depressed, lonely, and alienated.

Fortunately, we each have a divine guide who knows our true desires, and what will really make us happy. When we enter miracle-mindedness, we are in a position to converse with our guides and receive the advice we need to learn to use the supernatural power of our minds in ways that truly do benefit us. Further, with our permission, our guides can use the supernatural power of their own minds to protect us and help us along.

MIRACLES VERSUS MANIFESTATION

But if creating positive outcomes is just a matter of relentlessly focusing on the results we want and forgetting about those we don't, where does God come in? Can people who switch to a much more optimistic thought system create miraculous outcomes without calling upon, or even believing in, a higher power?

The answer is, I believe, a qualified yes. It would seem that the process of manifesting the object of one's belief and attention works in an automatic fashion. Drop the coin of your expectation into the great cosmic vending machine, and out comes a future circumstance closely resembling the one you anticipated. Gino, for example, did not have any particular faith in God at the time when he visualized his liver healing, yet it healed all the same.

But was this actually a *miracle* — an instance where a supernatural power interfered in the natural world? For purposes of this discussion, I am going to distinguish between the surprisingly good outcomes produced by shifting to a positive mental focus and those that result from the shift into miracle-mindedness. The former I will call *manifestation* and attribute to the divine power of the mind to unfold the future that interests it. The latter I will call *miracles*, and attribute to the intervention of an enlightened being acting on behalf of God. *Miracles* involve intelligent, goal-directed activity on the part of a supernatural being rather than simply the automatic process by which our ego-identified minds imagine the sort of world they've chosen to think real. When Hayden and Doris floated out to sea, for example, they didn't just think uplifting thoughts about being back on land and then find themselves on the beach. Some entity with supernatural powers intervened and towed them ashore. How do we access divine intervention of this sort? The first step is to go into miracle-mindedness.

The state I'm calling *miracle-mindedness* goes well beyond the focused concentration that sometimes allows us to manifest the outcomes we'd prefer. In a truly miracle-minded state we set aside all thought of controlling the outcome according to our own ideas, and we agree to go along with whatever outcome God knows to be best. This state of personal surrender is well expressed in the common prayer: "Not my will, but Thine oh Lord, be done in me and through me."

Miracles occur naturally the moment we truly turn the problem over to our higher power, setting aside our fears, resentments, and pet illusions about the way everything ought to be, and choosing instead to know and accept reality as God is Being It in the present instant. Think of Dona, consciously rejecting her prior fearful responses to her stepfather as a model for her response to the threat she faced in the laundry room. She centered herself in peace and found herself guided to a state of mind and way of behaving that allowed her to walk away from danger. Had she become fearful or angry instead, she would have mentally engaged with her would-be assailant instead of allowing herself to be guided to safety.

The startling reversals of fortune we call *miracles* represent divine solutions, in contrast to the sorts of outcomes we'd consciously choose to manifest when in ordinary ego consciousness. In a state of fear, we'd choose to defeat an enemy or portray ourselves as a victim. God has a better idea — that our so-called *enemy* go his or her way in peace, with no residual reason for guilt or fear remaining to trouble our minds.

I believe that this state of unconditional surrender to Reality is the reason so many of those who shared their miracle stories with me believed they were going to die but were perfectly okay with that possibility. Like Heidi, they were prepared to go along with whatever God thought best. And this total abdication of their individual will permitted their divine guides to intervene and help them actualize the future that was not only best for them, but also for everyone else involved.

Things to Think About

1) Worry only attracts the circumstances you worry about.

2) You can unwittingly allow yourself to be hurt just by believing yourself vulnerable.

3) Striving for the things your ego wants will never satisfy you.

Chapter Twelve

The Trap of the Ego Mind

Do you really believe you can plan for your safety
and joy better than He can? You need be neither
careful nor careless; you need merely cast your cares upon
Him because He careth for you.

— *A Course in Miracles*

In order to explain who our guides are, we'll have to examine the issue of who you and I are and how we come to be living in an illusory world that outpictures our thoughts. The spiritual perspective we're exploring asserts that the mind has two broad domains. The first, which I'll call the *ego mind*, comprises ordinary waking consciousness, the various sleep states, and the individual's personal unconscious. Most psychologists think that is all there is to the mind.

But many wisdom traditions recognize another, much larger aspect, sometimes called the *transpersonal mind*. It is associated with intuition, psychic abilities, higher consciousness, miracles and, ultimately, awareness of one's true relationship to God, the world, and all other beings. This is the part of the mind seekers of truth such as meditators, artists, philosophers, and scientists cultivate. It is the only aspect that is able to perceive things accurately and be genuinely objective. It is also the only part of the mind that is capable of love.

A THEORY OF HUMAN CONSCIOUSNESS

How did we wind up with our minds divided this way? The account *A Course in Miracles* gives of the human condition says that some of the Children of God were curious to know what it would be like to be separate from God and one another, so that they could use their free will to make up a world all their own. The goal of a separate existence was completely incompatible with reality, since we are created through the extension of God and can have no existence apart from God. Nevertheless, while separation could never be real, we were free to *dream* anything we wanted. And, according to the *Course*, that's exactly what you and I did and continue to do.

Our egos are the aspects of our minds to which we assigned the task of dreaming that we succeeded in separating from God. Egos generate the illusion of a world where God appears to be absent and, quite possibly, nonexistent. In this dream we play the role of God and arrogate to ourselves the right to say what everything means and what "ought to" happen (even though it seldom does).

Unfortunately, the illusory worlds we are making up are necessarily scary places to be. After all, God is Love. If you blot out your memory of Love, all that remains to work with is Love's imaginary opposite: fear. Thus, in the worlds we "separated" Children of God dreamed up, we seem to be vulnerable mortal creatures struggling to survive in an uncaring universe riddled with threats to our safety, health, prosperity, and continued existence. Ironically, we cling to our egos as our guides to this frightening experience they are making up as they go along.

Now, there isn't really anywhere to be other than in Heaven because God didn't create anything else. So we are eternally safe in Heaven, although when we look around ourselves through the distorting lens of our egos, everything looks strange and unfamiliar. That's because the ego always adds a little something to our perception of reality that isn't actually there, or it subtracts a little something that is. And since each ego has its own unique bias, no two personal illusions are exactly alike. No wonder we find it so hard to agree on anything! At the level of our ego minds, each of us has crafted a world that is uniquely chaotic, meaningless, and threatening. But since it is our own personal invention, we cherish and defend it nonetheless.

GOD SENT GUIDES TO WATCH OVER US

The *Course* says that it was perfectly all right with our Creator that some Children of God chose to fall asleep in Heaven and dream they were somewhere else. As Jesus points out, the Bible tells us that Adam fell asleep in Paradise, and there is nowhere any mention of his ever having woken up! In this view, everything that has happened since Paradise has been only a series of dreams.

But while God had no objection to our entertaining nightmares about being driven out of Paradise and having to scratch out a difficult existence on our own, our divine parent considerately assigned some of our siblings who remained Awake to watch over us while we slept. Their mission is to help us awaken when we've had our fill of the imaginary but nonetheless terrifying dream worlds we are making up to replace Heaven. Thus, whenever we elude our ego's vigilance and slip into the transpersonal aspect of our minds, our guides are quietly waiting there to educate, protect, and nurture us. But they are not authorized to interfere in our dreams without our permission.

So the person you take yourself to be is really only a character your ego made up so that you could take part in the consensual dream the sleeping Children of God are sharing. Nevertheless, when you identify with your ego, you think it is *you* and struggle passionately to defend and further its interests as if *you* had something to gain through doing so.

If you want to get a feel for what it's like to identify with your ego, think about how readily you took up roles in games as a child. While playing Monopoly, you may have been so involved with the fate of your game token that you actually felt sad when that tiny thimble was sent to jail or failed to pass Go and collect $200. In the same way you "became" a cowboy or a ballerina at will as a child, you've spent a lifetime perfecting your impression of the limited, mortal individual you are portraying today. But that isn't who you really are.

ILLUSION VERSUS REALITY

Given that this world we seem to see around us is actually only a product of our imaginations, is it really any wonder that whatever a Child of God habitually thinks about tends to manifest in his or her experience? Nonetheless, reality as God is Being It is going on right where we perceive only our ego's loveless illusions. An illusion is, after all, a distorted perception of something real. Just beneath the thin veneer of fear our egos project over everything we see is its divine reality.

Now, if our illusions are so scary and unsatisfying, you may be wondering why we don't all simply abandon our dreams and reawaken in Heaven. We are reluctant to do that because it would mean forgetting about the imaginary world we've been making up and the competitive games we've been playing here with our dreaming brothers and sisters. The price of our return to Heaven is that we must recognize that the world we presently see is only a figment of our imaginations.

We cherish the world we dreamed up because we made it. And we're in no hurry to end the dream because there is a fascinating game in progress within the larger consensual illusion — one in which everyone competes to be recognized as the most special and worthy of love. This idea that one Child of God could deserve more love than another is incomprehensible in Heaven, where all Children of God are loved equally and completely. But our egos are dreaming of a realm where everyone has to compete for recognition, and it seems like a shame to fold our hand when we still might win the jackpot of universal admiration our egos crave.

Of course, it isn't really possible to win the ego's game. The obsession with being best only leads to perpetual conflict and resentment. The transient sense of superiority we achieve in triumphing over another never satisfies us for long, and other egos are seldom disposed to acknowledge our superiority in any case. Still, as depressing as the specialness game is most of the time, our egos are so fixated on winning that it doesn't occur to us to give it up and "settle for" peace, equality, and infinite love.

Waking Up

Forgiveness is the key to releasing ourselves from our ego-identification so that we can reawaken in Heaven. It is essential to forgive our brothers and sisters for all of the "wicked" and "unfair" things we imagine they did to us in their efforts to win the specialness we wanted for ourselves. When we acknowledge that all of this drama is just a game — and indeed, one in which we've played dirty as often as anyone else — we are ready to release the ego's world with no hard feelings toward any of our former competitors. Now we affirm equality and truly "love our neighbors as ourselves."

The moment we release our grievances, we shift back into our right (transpersonal) minds, where we remember the eternal love we have for everything God created. And since love dissolves illusion, Heaven stands revealed right where our egos had been showing us only our own personal hell.

Indeed, whenever we decide to forgive someone who seems to be threatening us (whether physically, verbally, financially, psychologically, or in any other way), we slip back into our right minds. Looking out upon the world through the eyes of love, we instantly recognize our former enemy as a beloved brother or sister and rejoice at the meeting.

Now, doesn't that sound like what many of the people who shared their deliverance experiences did right before their situation took a "miraculous" turn for the better? When people like Ashley and Debra chose not to judge the men who threatened their lives, but rather to forgive them and love them without conditions, they recognized these men as beloved brothers and reminded them that they were their beloved sisters. Isn't it interesting that Brian Nichols actually called Ashley Smith his "sister in Christ"?

When someone averts disaster by momentarily transcending his or her ego to achieve miracle-mindedness, we think of the person as *lucky, blessed*, or perhaps, *clever*. When the person decides to remain in her or his right mind ever after, we call her or him *enlightened, Christ-like, Buddha-like, self-realized, awakened, Krishna-conscious, liberated, God-realized, cosmically-conscious*, and so forth. Individuals who achieve this level of awareness don't suddenly drop dead, or disappear, or ascend bodily into the sky, or anything like that. Unless they want to. They mostly just wake up to the fact that an infinitely loving Creator has given them the means to ensure their perfect safety by resting eternally in peace and love.

What happens to your ego when you awaken from illusion? The same thing that happens to any other dream when you wake up. It wasn't real to begin with, and the moment you stop imagining it, it isn't there anymore.

WHY THE EGO OPPOSES MIRACLES

I've said that divine guidance and divine intervention are available to those who truly turn within for help by entering a meditative state. So why is it that our ego minds do everything in their power to convince us not to do that?

First, *that's their assignment.* We specialized our egos to keep us so involved with their illusions that we would not remember God. In distracting us from awakening, they are just doing their job.

Second, *all egos are desperately afraid of God.* The part of your mind you specialized to function as an ego feels deeply threatened by Love because it believes it succeeded in separating from It. This leads it to imagine that God is mightily offended by its "betrayal" and just waiting to brutally punish it when you "die." After all, brutal punishment is what your ego thinks the people who offend *it* deserve. Having cut themselves completely off from God, egos create imaginary gods in their own images. Just like the egos that dreamed them up, these gods tend to be jealous, petty, and vindictive. Thoughts of love become even more distant as we work to placate these imaginary deities.

It follows that whenever you identify with your ego, *you believe God is out to get you*, and you want to avoid at all costs the transpersonal part of your mind that remembers God. That's why this ego-generated illusion we take to be reality is always pervaded with a sense of futility and ultimate doom. We unconsciously believe we have a powerful Enemy who will inevitably make us pay for our little adventures in the loveless and thoroughly unsatisfying imaginary worlds our egos have dreamed up.

It doesn't matter how strenuously some of us maintain our atheism, or how much the rest of us try to butter God up with personal sacrifices and declarations of everlasting devotion. All ego-identified individuals unconsciously believe that, sooner or later, they're going to die. And when they do, God is going to get them, and then there will be hell to pay!

VICTIMHOOD OR MIRACLES?

Now, the most common experience associated with identification with our ego is the perception of ourselves as *innocent victims*. All egos secretly believe they are guilty for having "betrayed" God and "usurped" God's creative power to make a world of their own. When you identify with your ego, *you* feel guilty, although you don't know why. It just feels as if you are somehow fundamentally bad, unworthy, and inadequate, and that no one could possibly love you if they knew the truth about you. We ego-identified individuals are obsessed with keeping this unworthiness out of consciousness. All we consciously recognize is that something is very wrong with us, and since we don't understand what it is, it can't very well be our fault. Thus, we are innocent victims.

This propensity to feel victimized is greatly enhanced by the fact that the ego projects the mental causes of events from our minds out onto the world and other people. This makes it very difficult to see that our problems have more to do with our angry, fearful thoughts than with the people or events that seem to be their cause.

But if the spiritual theory we're exploring is true, and

you're either creating, or at a minimum, acquiescing to what happens to you, how can you really be anyone's victim?

You can't.

Nevertheless, if you choose to believe you are, it will seem to be verified by your experience, just as evidence for anything else you decide to believe tends to be outpictured within your personal illusion. When you choose to view yourself as guilty and worthy of punishment, the fearful, angry thoughts in your mind are projected onto your environment, making it look and feel as if you're being persecuted by circumstances beyond your control or by others. That's why relieving a person's sense of guilt, as psychotherapists often do, can cause their physical symptoms, relationship problems, and other self-inflicted misfortunes to disappear.

The good news is that no one chooses their ego's hell over Heaven permanently. After all, you can change your mind about what to believe in an instant. And when you switch from thoughts of being punished and victimized to thoughts that are peaceful, loving, and forgiving, you yank the rug out from under any negative circumstance your ego's previous fearful or resentful thoughts were creating. Remember, physicists and spiritual adepts alike agree that time and space are ultimately illusory. Since only the present instant is real, all that matters is what you believe right now. Let's see how a profound shift in belief can instantly alter a long-standing physical condition.

CHERYL PREWITT: MISS AMERICA, 1980

In 1980 I remember seeing that year's Miss America, Cheryl Prewitt, interviewed on the *Merv Griffin Show*. This guest, who had recently been selected as one of America's most beautiful and accomplished young women, said that this title had been her goal since early childhood. When she was five years old, the family's milkman had told Cheryl that she would someday grow up to be Miss America, and she believed him!

Unfortunately, at age eleven Cheryl was involved in a major automobile accident. Among many other serious injuries, she had much of the flesh ripped off her face when she was thrown through a windshield, and several inches of bone had to be surgically removed where one of her legs was crushed. According to her doctors, she would bear the scars of this accident for the rest of her life. She would never walk again or be able to have children.

I recall that Merv commented on the quality of cosmetic surgery Cheryl must have received to restore her face to its present beauty. The young woman replied that she had never had any plastic surgery at all. The emergency room doctors had simply stitched her face together as best they could after the accident. She showed Merv that, underneath her makeup, her complexion was actually seamed with a network of faint scars from the 150 stitches it had taken.

Cheryl explained that through her faith in God and miracles, she achieved a phenomenal recovery. Despite the predictions of her doctors, she did regain the ability to walk, although one leg remained inches shorter than the other because of the bone that had been removed. This caused her to limp and necessitated her wearing a prosthetic shoe. Despite her awareness that people do not become Miss America if they limp through the bathing suit competition in a prosthetic shoe, this young woman never lost her conviction that she would someday win that title.

As a senior in high school, Cheryl said that some words she heard at a healing service convinced her that God had no reason to want her to suffer with a short leg. When she realized that this must be true, her short leg grew out to the same length as the other one. Despite the surgical, radiological, and photographic evidence that inches of bone had been removed, and that her injured leg had been significantly shorter, it was now the same length as the other. If I am remembering correctly, she went on to win Miss Congeniality in her first Miss America Pageant, and her Miss America title on her second attempt. Today Cheryl Prewitt Salem is a wife, a musician, and a minister. She has also borne three children.

I suspect that once Cheryl Prewitt became aware of her unconscious conviction that God must have a reason for punishing her with a short leg, this young woman was able to consider it rationally. How could it be that divine love could want one of Its creations to suffer? How could she be exempt from universal forgiveness? She realized that her physical limitations could not possibly represent the will of a loving God.

Further, if reality is God's will, how could her disability be part of reality? If God didn't will her to have a short leg, and she didn't will herself to have a short leg, how could she have a short leg? Once she realized she couldn't, she didn't.

It sounds to me as if Cheryl was initially afraid of God's will for her because of some sense of guilt or unworthiness.

Once she realized God wills only her happiness, she surrendered and was healed.

A miracle of this sort, where physical "reality" is dramatically changed in an instant, is hard for most people to credit. Yet if the perception we have of our physical body is really only our own personal dream, it should be no more difficult for a shift in perception to change it totally than it is to change it slightly. That's why there is no order of difficulties in miracles.

When we discard all of the limiting beliefs that are causing a physical problem, it should disappear, and only the vital healthy body that God is broadcasting as our own unique visibility and tangibility should remain. Similarly, when our fearful thoughts create danger in our environment, releasing them to enter miracle-mindedness should cause the threat to rapidly dissipate. Past thoughts cannot influence the present or the future unless we *believe* they can and thereby agree to let them.

Things to Think About

1) You have a right mind — the transpersonal one you share with God and all of God's creations — and a wrong mind, the ego you specialized to allow you to feel separate from, and more special than, everyone else.

2) When you are in your right mind, miracles occur naturally.

3) When you are in your right mind, your divine guide can direct and protect you.

4) Believe it or not, you may be unconsciously afraid of God and mistakenly believe your ego is protecting you by providing a state of mind where God cannot enter.

Chapter Thirteen

What Your Divine Guide Can Do for You

When you no longer perceive the world as hostile, there is no
more fear, and when there is no more fear, you think, speak,
and act differently. Love and compassion arise, and they affect
the world. Even if you find yourself in a conflict situation,
there is an outflow of peace into the polarities.

— *Eckhart Tolle*

Our divine guides are awakened brothers and sisters
who share and therefore think with the Mind of God
— as you and I once did, and as we will do again when we
lay aside our egos' dreams. These inner companions understand the way things really work in the universe, as well as
the way they look to you and me right now. They also know
that the events we experience are being generated by our
minds according to our beliefs. They can work miracles and
teach us to do so, too, because they realize that what we take
to be reality is really only a dream. After all, how hard is it to
alter a dream, once you realize that that's all it is?

I believe that when we slip into miracle-mindedness, we implicitly authorize our guides to do whatever is necessary to protect us and restore peace and harmony within our physical illusion. Our inner teachers' ultimate goal is to get us to the point where we wake up all the way and no longer need their help. Until we're ready to do that, their mission is to offer whatever assistance we are prepared to accept. With our permission, they will gently extricate us from terrifying situations we've unwittingly created and remind us how to use the power of Love to keep ourselves safe and fulfilled. There are a number of ways in which they can rescue us from self-created threats.

ELICITING HELP FROM OTHERS

Perhaps the major way in which our guides are able to help even those of us who don't realize we *have* a guide is by helping us to meet our needs. Let's say you have a problem and either formally pray for help or informally turn within for guidance. This authorizes your guide to act on your behalf by prompting others to come to your assistance. He or she may also use your openness to maneuver you into the vicinity of needed resources.

From your point of view, it may seem as if someone just happens along, sees your plight, and is moved to stop and help. Or that you encounter the very thing you've been seeking "quite by accident," as did Alana when she found those three dollars in the snow. Incidents like these are easily mistaken for lucky breaks. Few people realize that they may represent their guide's efforts to help them.

Our Guides Can Tell Us
What We're Doing Wrong

If we are unwittingly creating the problems that plague us through our misguided attitudes and beliefs, it may well be that the only way our higher power *can* help is by encouraging us to change our minds and see things differently. Neither God nor the guides sent to watch over us will undo circumstances that our own chosen beliefs are holding in place. To do so would violate our free will. Like a loving parent who will advise and help if asked but will not otherwise interfere, God and our guides let us decide when we want to listen and learn. Going into a meditative state is the evidence that we have given up on handling things according to our ego's advice, and we are truly turning the situation over to our higher power.

We've already seen many instances where the happy ending depended upon the ability and willingness of troubled individuals to speak and act as they were divinely inspired to do. Because our fearful, angry, ego-based interpretations are the real problem in any situation, our guide's advice to forgive and return to love often is the help for which we've been praying. If we ignore it, how can we expect anything to improve?

The following story is an excellent example.

Rob: Settling His Accounts

Rob was eager to accept an overseas assignment with Habitat International, but before he could leave the states, he needed $800 to pay off his debts. He planned to earn the money by working right up to the weekend before his move to Americus, Georgia, where he was to begin his training. Unfortunately, the firm that employed Rob was sold two months before he was scheduled to leave. When the new owners learned of his intention to quit, they immediately gave him two weeks' notice. This threw all of Rob's careful financial planning into chaos. Now how was he going to come up with the money to pay off his debts?

"To say I was angry doesn't even start to describe my feelings," Rob wrote me. "Here I was, off to go do something noble for the kingdom of God, and I was getting shafted! I blamed two men in particular and harbored true ill-will toward both. At the same time that I was muttering curses under my breath toward these two men (who in reality had nothing to do with my situation), I was also crying out to God for deliverance from my financial problems.

"In a moment of quiet prayer I heard Christ say, 'How can you enter into the temple when you are angry with your brothers? Go first to your brothers and seek forgiveness, then come to me with your requests.' I knew that this was truly from God and followed the instructions and explained my misplaced anger to both men and sought their forgiveness.

"Not five minutes had passed after talking to the second man than a friend I hadn't seen in about nine months walked into the store I was working in and asked me to go to lunch with her. After a pleasant lunch this friend (who knew nothing of my financial problem) handed me an envelope and said that God had been leading her to give this envelope for some time, but she had been resistant until that morning.

"Inside the envelope were sixteen \$50 bills, exactly the

$800 that was needed to get me out of debt. I wonder how often our anger and negativity block us from receiving the blessings that are already prepared for us."

How often, indeed! Rob could have prayed night and day for financial relief, but until he went into a state of miracle-mindedness, listened to his inner voice, and corrected the resentful thoughts that were blocking him from receiving his heart's desire, no divine assistance could have been received.

Rob's story illustrates the principle that in order for us to maintain someone else's guilt, we must make, and keep, ourselves miserable. As long as Rob wished to assert that he was the innocent victim of the men who laid him off, he couldn't afford to solve his financial problem. It would have undermined his whole argument for their guilt and let them off the hook — a thing he was initially unwilling to do. After all, how "cruel" and "inconsiderate" could their treatment of him have been if it didn't ultimately interfere with his happiness or success?

In order to "prove" their guilt, Rob had to have a serious financial problem to present in evidence against them. Otherwise, he'd be hating them for no reason, and that would amount to an unprovoked mental attack on two innocent people. None of us want to see ourselves as bad people, attacking others without justification. That would interfere with our fantasies of specialness.

Rob wisely sought divine guidance and chose to implement his inner teacher's advice to confess his error, forgive, and seek to be forgiven for his mental attacks. Prior to doing so, he could not receive the gift his friend had for him *because he didn't really want it.* What he wanted was to prove that he had been injured by the men who laid him off.

Notice, too, that the monetary gift was not being withheld by God, or Jesus, or his friend as some sort of punishment for Rob's resentful attitude. His resentful attitude was simply the evidence that he preferred to be "right" about his former bosses' guilt rather than to solve his financial dilemma. The universe respected his decision to portray himself as a victim until such time as he changed his mind.

OUR GUIDES CAN DIRECT OUR THOUGHTS

Another thing our guides can do if we will allow it is to unite their minds with our right mind and then direct that "melded" mind to embrace peace and believe in our highest possibilities. I suspect that is what happened to those people who found themselves endangered and said they "just knew everything was going to be all right," despite believing, at another level of consciousness, that that was just crazy.

Since belief is an essential aspect of manifestation, we need help when we can't bring ourselves to believe in our own good. Sometimes a friend or a therapist or a spiritual counselor is able to persuade us that we deserve to be happy, healthy, prosperous, and safe. By speaking divine truth to us, they can remind us that these things are God's will for us. But there's no time for consultation with human mentors in cases of accidents and assaults. That's when we truly need our inner teacher to join with us to manifest an outcome far better than any we could envision on our own.

This goes deeper than simply maintaining a positive outlook, which is important but is sometimes not enough. When difficulties overwhelm our personal ability to remain optimistic — such as during a frightening accident or attack — we can know that there is one more resource to turn to — our inner guide. God has sent a wise and loving companion to look after each of us. It only makes sense to avail ourselves of his or her help.

OUR GUIDES CAN WARN US AND DIRECT OUR ACTIONS

Our guides can also foresee our likely short-term future and read the thoughts of others involved in a situation. This allows them to warn us and prompt us to behave in ways that will avoid problems. Think of Mel being told to "move to the left" on that dark country road, or Liz having a disturbing fantasy about what would happen if she stopped to help people in a car wreck just a few minutes before encountering the identical situation in real life.

Guides can also direct us to act in ways that work to our advantage and open the hearts of erstwhile enemies. I suspect that that's what happened to Ashley when she was inspired to read *The Purpose-Driven Life* to Brian Nichols and to make him pancakes for breakfast. Even giving him her drugs was intended by her, and received by him, as a loving act. These responses seem to have been uniquely designed to touch the heart of her captor and induce him to shift from his ego to his right mind.

Even further, when we solicit their help, our guides can actually speak and act through our bodies, handling situations we could not presently handle on our own. What follows is a vivid example of how this works.

JOAN: FLIRTING WITH DISASTER

After hearing me speak about miracles at an "Anthropology of Consciousness" conference, Joan came up to share some astonishing deliverance experiences of her own. She said that as a young woman she had dated an ex-convict (whom I'll call Peter). Although she hadn't know it at the time, she later learned from police that Peter had served time for beating a woman to death and was suspected of being a serial killer. He had seemed nice enough, and Joan — young and idealistic — didn't believe in holding anyone's past mistakes against them. Whatever he had done, he had paid his debt to society. As far as she was concerned, that was the end of it.

For the first month or two, Peter appeared to be perfectly normal and pleasant. But then he began slipping into some sort of psychotic state. Joan doesn't know what the appropriate diagnosis would have been, but she suspects that he may have been bipolar (manic-depressive). She said that Peter gradually became extremely bizarre and frightening. He seemed obsessed with her, and it was impossible to get him to leave her alone. One day when she was over at his place he announced that he was going to kill her.

Peter knocked Joan to the floor with a powerful blow to the side of her head and then sat down on top of her supine body, pressing a pillow over her nose and mouth with one hand, while beating her brutally about the head with the other. Joan says that consciousness began to slip away, and she knew that she was about to die. However, that thought suddenly triggered an altered state.

"I'll have to back up a bit to explain why I responded the way I did," Joan told me. "Ever since I was a small child I've

always had this conviction that if I could just be in a peaceful, fearless state at the moment of death, everything would
somehow be all right. It had something to do with what I
thought would happen after death — by this means I would
move on to some better form of existence.

"I couldn't articulate it very well — especially when I
was little. I don't know how many times people have accused
me of being morbid because of my interest in death and
dying. But I wasn't being morbid, really. I just felt a spiritual
need to prepare for my own death. Dying well has always
seemed to me to be the culmination of a life well lived.

"Now, a year or so before this incident, a psychic had told
me that if I didn't learn to meditate, I was going to die. I certainly didn't understand her to mean anything like this mur-
derous attack — just that I was scattered and living in my
head in a way that was very unhealthy. Anyway, for a number of months I had been studying meditation.

"When Peter was pounding on me, and trying to suffo-
cate me, I realized that this must be the moment of death I
had always hoped to handle well. So I went into a meditative
state at once and became totally calm and one-pointed. The
fear I had felt drained away, and I was totally at peace with
whatever was to happen.

"But at the same time I was becoming peaceful and detached, my arms and legs began flailing wildly. It's strange,
but while my mind was so very calm, my body became incredibly powerful and active. I felt like a detached observer
as my body kicked and punched and scratched at Peter like
it was possessed. Once I had fought Peter off enough to get
the pillow off my face, I began biting him savagely. I didn't

know I could bite that hard! Under other circumstances, I would be afraid of breaking my teeth right off.

"As unlikely as it seems, I went from being helpless and practically unconscious to hurting Peter so bad that he got off me and backed away, looking scared. And somehow the pain I had inflicted on him temporarily shook him out of whatever blood lust he had been into. He calmed down a bit and lost interest in trying to kill me.

"Peter said that when I started really fighting back, I had been so strong that he had been afraid I would actually beat him to death. I had had a glass or two of wine earlier that evening, and he told me that he thought that if I hadn't had that wine to slow me up, I would have killed him for sure. Now, he was crazy, so I don't know how accurate his impression was. All I know is that once I entered that meditative state, I seemed to access incredible strength and skill as a fighter. I went from half-dead to being able to beat off the attack of a man much bigger than myself."

Joan finally escaped from Peter that night by climbing out a bathroom window. She reported the assault to the police, who told her about Peter's criminal past and their suspicion that he had beaten a number of women to death in addition to the one for whose murder he had been convicted. Unfortunately, Peter had managed to disappear by the time the police went looking for him, and he used his freedom to stalk his former girlfriend with the intention of finishing what he had started. Joan's long nightmare only ended after the following extraordinary incident.

"Peter had been following me for weeks, and he finally cornered me in an isolated alley. He seemed full of glee over the fact that he was finally going to kill me. He closed in on me warily and when he was close enough, he made his lunge.

"I saw no hope of defending myself from his attack. However, some time before this my meditation teacher had taught the class a technique from martial arts for drawing up protective power. It involves raising the cupped right hand, in front of your body, as if lifting a shield of energy from your lower chakras to the top of your head. As Peter lunged for me, I stilled my mind in meditation and made the necessary gesture to invoke protection.

"To my astonishment, his attack was deflected in midair! I never touched him, but instead of connecting with my body, the trajectory of his leap changed suddenly at a 90-degree angle. He went flying as if he'd been snatched up and then tossed aside by some giant, and he landed in a heap a few yards away looking scared out of his wits. Then he got up and ran away. I'm glad to say that I've never seen him since."

In his delusional state, Joan's ex-con boyfriend evidently took pleasure in his easy "victories" over women. These women surely didn't *want* to engage in a physical contest with him, but they nonetheless dutifully played out their assigned role as victim when he thrust it upon them. More than likely, they didn't realize they had any other alternative to becoming terrified and vainly struggling and dying at this lunatic's hands.

Joan was the exception. Instead of joining in the battle by trying to best her assailant physically, verbally, or psychologically (through guilt), she simply acknowledged that she could not possibly solve the problem on her own, withdrew into peace, and left her defense to her higher power. In effect, she asserted her God-given right to be free of interference and left it to the "authorities" to enforce it.

Her guide evidently felt authorized by her request to respond by taking over her body and fighting her battle for her. Several weeks later during the second attack, when Joan ritually drew up protective spiritual energy after being cornered in the alley, she once again consciously "turned the situation over to her higher power," only to have an invisible force snatch her assailant out of midair and cast him aside.

This is an amazing story, but I also have my own experience of letting my guide take over my actions when I was at a loss about what to do.

LAURA: MEETING MY INNER THERAPIST

While directing a program for hospitalized female mental patients who had been sexually abused as children, I worked with a very disturbed woman whom I'll call Laura. In addition to bipolar disorder, she had a severe case of borderline personality disorder and was a recovering alcoholic. She had an extensive history of suicidal behavior and assaults upon others, and her children had been removed from her care as a result of the sadistic physical and emotional abuse she had inflicted upon them while in psychotic states.

One Sunday afternoon while I was at home idly flipping through channels on the TV, I received a call from Laura, who was now seeing me for psychotherapy on an outpatient basis. I picked up the phone and then snatched it away from my ear as she began screaming obscenities. As Laura continued to rave, it became clear that she had gone into a psychotic state characterized by intense paranoia. She was now threatening to kill me, and then herself, having decided that, as her therapist, I was personally responsible for all of her unhappiness.

Many anxious thoughts flashed through my mind. "She's off her medication. I should have the police pick her up before she hurts herself or someone else. But how can I do that when I don't know where she is?" (I knew that Laura's home phone had been disconnected for nonpayment of the bill, so she couldn't be calling from there, and in her present paranoid state she would almost certainly refuse to tell me where she was.)

I attempted to speak, but Laura simply shouted me down. How was I going to help her if I couldn't even get a word in? I searched my mind for anything I had learned in the course of my professional training that might help in this situation and came up empty. I simply had no idea what to do.

Since my clinical training failed to provide any useful guidelines, I turned next to my spiritual training. The first thing to do was to calm down and come back into the truth. What was the truth here? The truth, I concluded, was that I was just a limited human being who did not know what to do. However, it was also true that I could turn to my higher power for help if I chose to do so.

"God, this is your client," I said inwardly. "I think you'd better do something about this, because I sure as hell don't know what to do!"

Having said this, I figured that I should probably try to calm down and go into a meditative state in case my higher power had any bulletins for me. If I were in a peaceful state of mind, some sense of ease might begin to penetrate Laura's terror. She would have to stop screaming to catch her breath at some point, and if she didn't hang up first, I might just manage to jump into the conversation. I had no idea what I would say, but hopefully that would be clearer when the time came. As Laura continued her litany of paranoid threats and accusations, I cleared my mind to enter meditation.

The next thing I knew, I was totally absorbed in a scene from *Conan the Barbarian*! Before picking up the phone, I had evidently flipped the television to a station playing that movie. I can only guess that my eyes must have been resting on the TV set in front of me while I was on the phone, and somehow it had happened that I had become totally engrossed in the movie.

I suddenly awoke to the fact that I had been concentrating on the film as though it were the most fascinating thing I had ever seen. Although I had little sense of time, my recent memory was filled with idle thoughts about Arnold Schwarzenegger's impressive physical endowments: "Holy mackerel, look at the muscles on that guy! Can that be healthy? He must be on steroids." It was clear that my total absorption in the movie had been going on for at least five minutes, and maybe much longer.

I was electrified by the realization that I was on the phone with a suicidal client and here I was watching television. "Oh my God, Carolyn!" I thought. "This might just be the worst thing you've ever done in your life!" This was rapidly succeeded by other thoughts: "Don't take time to beat yourself up now, stupid! You've got to get back to Laura and see if there's anything you can do to save the situation. Maybe she didn't notice that you weren't paying attention. Yeah, right! A paranoid client didn't notice she'd been ignored for five minutes. Buy a clue, Carolyn."

I jerked back to the phone call in a panic and was shocked to hear a strange voice talking in my living room. I was further astonished to realize that it wasn't a strange voice at all — it was my voice, speaking calmly into the phone! While I had been watching television, my mouth had been talking, and I had no idea what it had been saying. I felt that I had now truly entered the Twilight Zone.

As I started surfing on a new wave of fear, I remembered that I had asked my higher power to take over. Just maybe, it had done so. Maybe I should calm down and find out what was going on before panicking further. After all, I thought reasonably, there would be plenty of time for panic later.

When I tuned in to the discussion between the voice and my client, it was a lot like overhearing the conversation at the next table in a restaurant. I initially had trouble making sense of what was being said because I was entering in the middle. However, it soon became apparent that the voice was offering an interpretation of the reason Laura had gotten so upset. I was unaware of the recent events in Laura's life to which it alluded, but as the reason was explained, I remember thinking, "Yeah! I'll bet that's right. That's just the sort of thing that would set her off."

From the other end of the line, I heard Laura say, "Yeah! I'll bet that's it, Carolyn. That must be what happened." I was amazed to see that she was now completely calm and co-operative. The psychotic intensity I had heard in Laura's voice earlier had been replaced by focused interest and enthusiasm. And, clearly, she thought I was the one talking.

Laura asked a number of questions that the voice answered insightfully and without hesitation. It ultimately reminded Laura of "our" scheduled appointment the next day and offered a few sensible suggestions for managing her anxiety until then. At the conclusion of the call, Laura thanked me profusely and apologized very sincerely for the terrible things she had said earlier. This paranoid client who always noticed and expressed suspicion about every detail of my dress, speech, and behavior was completely convinced that I had been talking to her! Then we both hung up, and I had my voice back.

The individuals whose miracles we've discussed all seem to have followed this same pattern of accepting their own powerlessness and retreating into inner peace to seek a new perspective. This authorized their guides to direct them through danger or to actually take over and steer the car, install the beaver pond, tow them to shore, or do whatever else was necessary to rescue them.

It has often been said that "God helps those who help themselves." I think this is frequently misinterpreted to mean that you should make up your own mind about how to understand and handle a situation, and then you should proceed, relying upon God merely for backup. Supposedly, God will then join in to manifest the solution you and your ego came up with.

In reality, if you want a miracle, you must abandon the idea that you and your ego have the resources to solve the problem on your own. Acknowledging your powerlessness, you must turn within for guidance and then do what your guide proposes.

Only those who implement divine guidance are truly "helping themselves" as the maxim suggests.

Here is one more story to consider.

SAM: TAKING A COURSE

Sam was just completing his doctorate in psychology when he discovered that the rare autoimmune disease that had nearly killed him ten years earlier had come back. After extensive tests, he was informed one morning by his physician that his only chance for survival was to enter the hospital immediately for intensive chemotherapy.

Sam had spent six months in the hospital the last time, and he had had several rounds of chemotherapy. The prospect of further agonizing treatment was more than he could face.

Meditating upon his choices, Sam's initial reaction of "Why is God doing this terrible thing to me?" gave way to acceptance and surrender. After all, it was God's universe, and who was Sam to tell the Creator how to run it? Sam concluded that it was ultimately up to God whether he would live or die — not to some medicine or doctor. He informed his physician that he would not be seeking further treatment.

Having made the decision to leave his fate in God's hands, Sam felt oddly peaceful. He awaited developments with a sense of calm detachment. His young son was visiting that day, and Sam found that he was able to put aside his personal concerns and cheerfully devote himself to the Indian dish they had looked forward to preparing together.

That evening, Sam received a phone call from a man he

knew slightly through a mutual friend. The caller, a psychologist named Jim, said that he had heard some time ago that Sam was seriously ill, and that for weeks he had been hearing a voice in his head instructing him to call Sam and offer to heal him.

Jim said that as a student of *A Course in Miracles*, he assumed that he was hearing the voice of the Holy Spirit. He explained that he had not called sooner because there had seemed to be little point, knowing as he did that Sam was intensely skeptical about the possibility of spiritual healing. However, the voice had been so insistent today that Jim had decided to make the call just to get it to leave him alone.

Sam was astonished by the coincidence of his decision to leave his life or death up to God and the immediate offer of spiritual healing. Years earlier, Sam had briefly examined *A Course in Miracles*, and he had not thought much of it. As a Jew, he had found it difficult to relate to the Christian terminology. As a scientist, he thought its promise to teach people to perform miracles was preposterous.

Nevertheless, in the present instance, Sam couldn't see that he had anything to lose by meeting with the caller, and just maybe he would have something to gain. Why the Holy Spirit (assuming that it existed) would be going out of its way to help a Jew who didn't even believe in it, Sam couldn't imagine, but he felt he might as well look into it.

Sam and Jim set up a series of meetings that went on for months. Sam found his would-be healer to be a brilliant but stubborn man. Although Jim did some energy work on him, most of their time together was spent in heated debate over Jim's contention that Sam himself must be creating the illness at an unconscious level. Sam began reading the *Course* and discovered that it now made a lot more sense. He *did* have a habit of thinking negative thoughts, and once he realized the influence this must be having on his health, Sam changed his thinking, and the illness remitted. A few months later he was well again.

There are a few things I'd like to highlight in Sam's story. First, while the *offer* of healing is suggestive of help from some supernatural source, the actual healing depended upon Sam's change of mind. If Sam had steadfastly maintained his original skepticism, or had been unwilling to understand his own role in creating his illness, it is likely that no actual healing would have occurred. Jim was guided to encourage Sam to perceive his problem in a different way. By changing his destructive thoughts, Sam almost certainly healed himself. The only supernatural element seems to have been the inner voice that prompted Jim to share his knowledge with Sam at precisely the time Sam had slipped into a state of miracle-mindedness.

However, while it is true that Sam had to surrender to God before his healing could begin, it is important for me to add that I'm not advocating that sick people abandon their medical treatment — just that they recognize that physical treatments are not really the level at which healing is effected. Ultimately, it is the mind that causes sickness, and a change of mind that heals it.

Nonetheless, certain medical treatments produce beneficial effects that support the body in healing itself because of our consensual illusion regarding the way in which bodies function. Further, a physician or healer often supplies loving concern where it is badly needed and supports the patient's belief that healing is to be expected. All of these factors facilitate the change of mind that creates healing.

Finally, Jim said that he'd been hearing a voice in his head urging him to call Sam and offer to heal him for weeks, but on that particular day it had been so insistent that he'd acted. This is reminiscent of Rob's friend, who'd been prompted by divine guidance to give him $800 but had resisted doing so for weeks. Both finally acted at precisely the time the intended recipient of their help was in a state of mind that made it possible for them to receive the gift. I believe these are examples of the way our guides unite with our minds to promote behavior that is uniquely appropriate. In the next chapter we'll explore some of the ways our guides get their points across to those who are receptive.

Things to Think About

1) Your inner guide shares the Mind of God and wants only to help you awaken to your own power, innocence, and invulnerability.

2) Being a master of the time/space illusion, your guide can foresee what is likely to be your immediate future, warn you of potential problems, direct you toward responses that will bring success, and even physically protect you when necessary — but only with your permission!

Chapter Fourteen

Hearing Your Inner Voice

The Inner Voice That Speaks for God, Intuition, which is
nothing less than God in us, silently awaits our recognition
and cooperation.

— *Ernest Holmes*

If you aren't aware of having an inner guide, it's only because you haven't learned to distinguish her or his input
from the many and much louder voices of your ego. Your
ego is actually composed of a number of subpersonalities,
each of which embodies a particular way of being that you
embraced at one time or another as your personality was developing. Some of them are pretty childish, and each represents a distinct point of view that may conflict with the
perspectives of other subpersonalities. When these subpersonalities compete to assert their unique "spin" on events, it
can seem as though you've got an argumentative committee
in your head criticizing everything you say, do, and think.

For instance, a university student working against a deadline to complete a research paper might be aware of one stream of consciousness saying: "I can't believe how long I put this off! Now I'll never get it done on time. I'm lazy and incompetent and at this rate, it won't be long before everybody knows it! Why the hell did I go to that party last night when I should have been working on this? Grow up, dammit!"

Alternating with this critical monologue may be the voice of a subpersonality with a very different point of view: "Boy, I really got wasted last night! What a blast! And I think that new girl wants to hook up with me. Maybe I should give her a call right now and see if she wants to meet me for lunch. I can knock off this paper when I get home. Don't forget, 'All work and no play makes Jack a dull boy.'"

Does this sort of inner conflict sound at all familiar? Perhaps you can see why trying to follow your ego's advice is so crazy-making. Every time you do what one subpersonality wants you to, you are inevitably outraging several others. Further, the ones that aren't getting their way often refuse to cooperate with the one that is. Decide in favor of doing your work and the part of your ego that wants to go out on a date may distract you with sexual fantasies to the point where the afternoon is wasted anyway.

The Voice That Speaks for God

Amid the clamor of your ego's many voices is the calm, quiet one that expresses God's will through the voice of your divine guide. It's the easiest voice to ignore, since your guide seldom speaks at all unless invited to do so. And even then, you'd have to withdraw attention from your ego in order to hear your guide.

Inner guidance is usually extremely subtle. Most of the time, we benefit from it without ever recognizing its source. It seems as if a terrific idea just occurs to us, and we think, "Hey! I must be smarter than I thought!" Getting in touch with your guide isn't so much about having an extraordinary new experience as about recognizing the significance of one so totally familiar that you never really thought about it. Your guide has been with you from birth, and in quiet moments you've had innumerable conversations with her or him without realizing it.

Nevertheless, once you begin to focus on the process, it isn't all that hard to distinguish the voice of your divine guide from those of your subpersonalities. That's because your ego and your guide hold diametrically opposed views on most subjects. The voices themselves may not feel very different — they all pretty much seem like you, thinking or talking to yourself. But the content of their messages is like night and day.

Distinguishing Normal Ego Voices and Mental Illness from Divine Guidance

Before we explore the ways you can differentiate your ego's many voices from that of your guide, it's important to note that some forms of mental illness involve inner voices. In psychosis, it is believed that split-off subpersonalities that seem alien to the disturbed individual's will sometimes masquerade as other beings that can speak to them in their minds and control their thoughts. These pathological sub-personalities may foster grandiosity, or verbally abuse and persecute the person. They sometimes even order people to commit acts of violence against themselves or others.

Egos are never wise or genuinely kind, but the more they divorce themselves from reality and insist upon their own unique "take" on things, the more pathological they become. How can you tell whether a profound shift in perception should be ascribed to your divine guide or to a severely disturbed aspect of your ego?

Look at the view of reality it supports. The companion spirit God sent to advise and nurture you is the emissary of Love. He or she will never belittle you or advise you to punish yourself or attack someone else — except possibly in self-defense. And as we've seen from the miracle stories in this book, fighting back is seldom a guide's preferred method of handling even a deadly attack. Unconditional love for you and everyone else is the hallmark of guidance.

Your ego is bent upon proving that you are special. Any inner voice that tells you that you have a right to resent someone else, or that you are either more or less deserving than others, must be your ego.

If you hear voices in your mind that make you feel exalted or that leave you frightened and confused, seek professional help from a psychiatrist, psychologist, social worker, emergency room doctor, clergyperson, or hotline. And don't give up until you obtain effective treatment. There are many new medications and therapies that can be of enormous help to people plagued by destructive ego voices, and there is absolutely no need to suffer in silence.

CHARACTERISTICS OF DIVINE GUIDANCE

Charitable Attitude

Your inner teacher has a characteristically charitable attitude that the ego's many voices lack. It stands for universal innocence and is always kind and respectful to you and everyone else. Any stream of thought that belittles anyone or projects blame cannot be the voice of guidance.

While your inner teacher may sometimes be painfully direct, comments that constitute guidance are consistently fair and constructive rather than abusive and shaming. Remember Mel's conversation with the voice that told him to move to the left? It did not hesitate to point out his stubbornness, but even Mel recognized that as fair criticism.

Calm

The voice that speaks on behalf of God will also be calm and confident. Streams of thought that excite fear by "catastrophizing" about the danger you are in, or the trouble you have caused, can only be generated by the ego. My panicky thoughts when I caught myself watching television instead of helping Laura clearly reflected my ego's perspective. They asserted that I had done something catastrophically awful, called me "stupid," and generally laid a major guilt trip on me. This hectoring tone is typical of the ego's disorganized response to an emergency. Frightened and not knowing what to do, it casts around for someone to blame. The true self is always a handy target.

Similarly, excitement is simply fear mixed with hope.

Your ego craves it, but your guide wants to reintroduce you to the simple joys of peace and love and deep fulfillment.

Tolerance

Where diversity of any kind is concerned, egos are fundamentally intolerant and highly invested in getting other people to see things *their* way. In contrast, our guides generally display little interest in the possible mistakes of other people. They are there to help us awaken, and they know that criticizing others is just our ego's way of distracting *us* from our own need for mental correction. Since our own minds are the only things we actually *can* change, this makes excellent sense.

Your guide believes that all people are the equally precious and innocent Children of God. Everyone is entitled to make his or her own decisions and experience the consequences of those decisions. In this view, while there is one Truth, there are many ways of approaching it. No religion or way of life is right for everyone. The object is to find what works for you and then, perhaps, to share your discoveries with others who express an interest. There is no legitimate reason for interfering with people who make different choices, unless those choices lead to criminal behavior that impinges upon the freedom and well-being of others. Your guide respects your right to decide things for yourself, even when that means ignoring his or her advice.

A New Perspective or New Information

Another characteristic of the voice of real guidance is that it may be surprising — so much so that in some cases what your guide has to say may at first seem to be "coming out of left field." This is because his or her understanding of the situation is so very different from the way your ego has led you to view it. Working from an entirely different set of premises, your inner teacher arrives at a different conclusion about what the problem really is.

For example, I recall once asking my guide: "If, as you say, I have the power to work miracles, could I prevent war in the Persian Gulf?"

"Why would you want to?" came the prompt reply.

This seemed so bizarre that I couldn't believe I had heard right.

"Why would I want to prevent a war?" I returned with heavy irony. "Aren't you the guy they used to call the Prince of Peace? Surely this can't be that hard to follow! Am I going too fast for you here?" (As you have probably gathered, my guide has a great deal to put up with.)

Despite my ironic tone, my inner voice went on to patiently educate me about the value of free will, pointing out that I had always "enjoyed" the freedom to screw up my life in whatever way I wished, and that I had learned a great deal through my mistakes. If other people wanted an opportunity to learn through their own mistakes, why would I presume to deny their right to the same kind of education?

My guide said that if enough people wanted a war, there would be a war. If I didn't care to be involved in it, I was free to dream up some other experience for myself, but it was not appropriate to condemn or interfere with others on the grounds that I knew better than they what experiences they should have. I could try to persuade people to settle their differences peacefully, but in the final analysis, the decision about what to do was theirs. I would have to be satisfied knowing that whatever happened, everyone would learn from it.

How Divine Guidance Is Experienced

How does your guide communicate with you? It depends upon what you're receptive to. Here are some of the ways your guide may employ.

An Inner Voice

Your guidance may come through as an inner voice articulating an important message. For example, a publishing executive named Jan says that when her boyfriend proposed marriage, she heard a voice in her head shout, "No!" so loud she was surprised the guy didn't hear it himself. She went ahead and married him anyway, and wound up wishing she hadn't.

Author and spiritual teacher Marianne Williams says that she was once in an automobile accident where her vehicle was completely totaled. As her car went out of control and all hell was breaking loose around her, she heard a voice in her mind say, "You will not be taken." She walked away from the crash uninjured.

An "Inspired" Idea

Often, divine inspiration reaches us in the form of a new idea that seems to spontaneously arise in our minds when we're deeply relaxed. When you have a sudden insight that answers a troubling question, there's a good chance your guide has just gotten through to you.

Indeed, sometimes when our guides can't reach us in a waking state, inspiration slips past the ego's censorship in dreams. For example, the configuration of the carbon ring was discovered by a chemist who dreamt of a serpent biting its own tail. And in the nineteenth century, the sewing machine was invented by Elias Howe after he dreamt of a knight carrying a lance with a hole at its tip. (All previous efforts to develop a sewing machine had failed because they attempted to use ordinary sewing needles, with the hole for thread opposite the end that pierced the cloth.) Many people routinely ask for guidance in dreams each night before they go to sleep.

A Perceptual Shift

Guidance frequently takes the form of a shift in perspective. A situation we're in begins to appear in a different light, and the new point of view makes a loving, humorous, or assertive response seem more appropriate than whatever reaction the ego had in mind. An "enemy" is reconceptualized as a frightened and confused friend who is trying to get her needs met in an inappropriate way. It suddenly occurs to us to see a conflict from the other person's point of view. Something we regarded as "impossible" no longer looks so intimidating.

Channeling or Overshadowing

While most of the people who shared their deliverance stories with me followed inner promptings, some felt as if a higher power actually took control, speaking and acting in their place to handle a situation they might not have been able to cope with otherwise. My experience when my guide spoke to my client Laura for me is a good example. When you go into your right mind, it is possible for your companion spirit to express through you when appropriate.

A Gut Feeling

So-called gut feelings may represent guidance as well. Sometimes we experience an upwelling of tears and a feeling of great poignancy when we think or hear a sentiment that deeply resonates with us at the level of our souls. That's why people cry at weddings.

Some folks get goose bumps when they encounter an important truth. Others experience a sense of ease and expansion when they contemplate a course of action that is in alignment with the goals of their souls. And, of course, there is a corresponding prickly, cold, or clenched sensation that sometimes sweeps over us when we think or hear about something we'd do well to avoid. These and other physical sensations are subtle and fleeting, but they provide valuable guidance to those who learn to pay attention to them.

A Synchronous Experience

As I mentioned earlier, spiritual guidance can also take the form of meaningful coincidences. I don't know whether our guides actually orchestrate the co-occurrence of certain events in order to make a point, or they simply prompt us to notice existing coincidences that can be used to carry a message. But whenever we experience a really startling coincidence, it's a good idea to consider the possibility that our guide is attempting to tell us something.

We may be wishing we knew what to think or do when some significant words on a billboard catch our eye, or we may find the answer we've been seeking in a phrase spoken by a passerby.

For example, my husband became concerned about his eyesight when it was slow to return to normal after cataract surgery. As he was gazing out the window of a restaurant thinking about this, his eyes came to rest upon the address of the building across the street: 2020 Wilshire Boulevard. He immediately felt comforted, and sure enough, his vision improved to the 20/20 level a short time later. Had his eyesight not been about to improve, I suspect his guide would not have prompted him to notice the relationship between his concerns and the address.

While synchronous experiences often arise spontaneously, you can also ask your guide to communicate with you in that way. One technique is to ask for guidance, hold your question in mind, and then open a spiritual volume at random and read the first paragraph your eye falls upon. Here is another example.

MARY: ALL DRESSED UP AND NOWHERE TO GO

A former student of mine felt a need to relocate, but she didn't know where to go. Not wanting to make a mistake, she prayed for guidance. Was it only a coincidence that she began encountering the name *Santa Fe* all over the place?

Mary says that she would be driving along wondering where to move and would look up and discover that she was crossing Santa Fe Street. She would idly glance around in a café while pondering the move and notice a poster for the Santa Fe Opera Company on the wall. It began to seem as if every time she turned on her television, someone was talking about Santa Fe, and friends kept mentioning it, too.

After several weeks of this sort of thing, Mary was pretty well convinced that Santa Fe was the answer she'd been seeking, but she was still afraid to trust that she was reading the signs correctly. After all, she had never been to Santa Fe — or even to New Mexico for that matter. She wasn't about to relocate there without definite knowledge that this was really divine guidance. Driving home one evening from the hospital where she'd been working as a counselor, she really laid it on the line.

"I know you're trying to get through to me," Mary told her guide, "but I can be pretty dense, and I'm afraid of making a big mistake. I'm going to need you to make the answer really obvious." As an afterthought she added, "And don't forget that I'm a little nearsighted. If you're planning to show me the name of the place in written form, you're going to have to write *big*!"

Just then clanging bells and flashing lights forced her to halt at a railroad crossing. A locomotive with a string of five freight cars in tow slowly huffed past. Emblazoned in huge letters on the side of each car was the legend *Santa Fe*.

"Alright, already!" Mary laughed. "That's big enough for even me to see! Santa Fe it is!" She paid the city a brief visit and liked what she saw well enough to move there. Twelve years later she is still delighted with her decision.

JASON AND ARNIE: LISTEN FIRST, JUDGE SECOND

My husband, Arnie, is also a psychologist, and he tells of a client who was grappling with a difficult problem in therapy. At one point during their session, the young man — whom I'll call Jason — dropped into a meditative silence, staring off into space as he contemplated the ramifications of an important decision facing him. After a few moments, he startled Arnie by quietly announcing, "There's a being here with us in the room."

Asked to explain, Jason continued, "It's like a light. It seems to want to help me with my problem."

Arnie went along with this, asking, "How will it be able to help you?"

"I don't know," Jason replied.

"Why don't you ask it and see what it says," Arnie suggested. Jason listened inwardly while continuing to gaze at a point across the room. Then his eyes began to move. "Oh! It's trying to show me where to find the answer. It moved over there by those books. It says that the answer I need is in one of them."

"Which one?" asked Arnie.

"It seems to be that fat blue one — the third book down in the middle stack. Now the light is all around it."

Arnie went over and retrieved the volume indicated from among the fifty-odd books and journals stacked haphazardly on his worktable. "Do you know what book this is?" he inquired.

Jason replied that he didn't — just that the light had said it contained the answer he was seeking. Arnie asked Jason to find out where in the book they were supposed to look. Jason checked within and confidently rattled off a page and then a paragraph number. Arnie handed him the volume and suggested that he take a look.

Turning to the designated page and paragraph, Jason began to read aloud. Arnie said that a chill went up his spine as his client read off a passage that offered an illuminating insight into the very question they had been discussing. Jason looked up in wonder.

"That's it! That's exactly what I needed to know! Hey, what book is this anyway?" Turning it over in his hands, Jason discovered what Arnie already knew — appropriately enough, it was *A Course in Miracles*.

In this story, Arnie's open-minded and inquisitive reactions offer a good model for your own investigations into guidance. When Jason began talking about a "being" in the room, Arnie had no idea whether his client was having a spiritual experience or just fantasizing in an irrational, and possibly delusional, manner. Where another therapist might have quickly put a stop to this sort of thinking, Arnie was willing to reserve judgment and see where it led.

This is a very important point to emphasize. If you embark upon your search for guidance using all of your critical faculties from the get-go, you will surely fail. That's because your critical faculties belong to your ego. The fact that you are being cautious and judgmental indicates that you are identified with this false sense of self and not available to communicate with your inner guide.

I'm not suggesting that you *never* subject your guidance to rational scrutiny. Just that you put judgment "on hold" until you emerge from meditation. You'll never actually be *in* meditation as long as you try to bring judgment along with you.

Simply play along with whatever arises in consciousness once you are in a meditative state, whether it be ideas, words, images, memories, physical sensations, or anything else. Note what you are experiencing, ask for more information, and then wait patiently for the answers to come. Anything you experience may be significant.

DISCOVERING YOUR GUIDE'S VOICE THROUGH MEDITATION

How can you learn to hear your guide's voice? Like most skills, this is an area where practice makes perfect, and the best way to practice is through regular meditation. You wouldn't expect to sit down at a piano for the first time and play a beautiful sonata, and you shouldn't expect to confidently pick out your inner teacher's voice on the first try, either.

A Course in Miracles says that the voice of your guide is as loud as your willingness to hear it. When you are in mortal danger, your willingness to receive guidance may instantly become all-consuming. However, we don't put much effort into things we aren't convinced are possible. For that reason, it's a good idea to practice miracle-mindedness and to try contacting your companion spirit before emergencies arise. Your success in small things will encourage you to turn within for help when the stakes are higher.

It's been said that *prayer* is talking to God and *meditation* is listening to God. As we've seen, prayer alone is seldom sufficient for creating miracles because we can utter the words of a prayer while in a state of consciousness that is far from miracle-mindedness. Of course, simply uttering a prayer tends to draw you into an expanded state of consciousness, so it's always worth the effort to pray, even if you can't meditate as well. Nevertheless, since transforming a dangerous situation often depends upon one's ability to follow inner guidance, simply telling God what you think you need doesn't necessarily help. Remember Rob's story? He was praying for financial assistance, but simultaneously blocking his fulfillment through his resentment toward the men who fired him. It was not until he listened for guidance that he was able to receive the advice about forgiving them, and clear the path to the blessings being held in store for him.

The meditative state that allows you to communicate with your guide is actually a very simple and natural activity that everyone engages in from time to time throughout the day. Have you ever spent a few minutes gazing idly into the middle distance with unfocused eyes and nothing in particular going through your mind? That is a form of meditation.

There are many types of meditation, but all of them involve a resolute turning away from the ego's incessant chatter in order to experience a different, more peaceful form of consciousness. Nevertheless, approaches that do not emphasize that guidance is available do not actively encourage us to seek and find it.

For example, many people suffering from chronic pain are receiving great benefit from a process developed by Dr. Herbert Benson called the "relaxation response."[1] This highly effective technique for stilling the mind was borrowed from Eastern spiritual practices, but all spiritual context has been stripped from the meditation in order to make it more generally acceptable in the West.

Patients practicing the relaxation response shut out their egos by silently repeating a syllable. As a result of separating themselves from their egos, they slip into a peaceful state of meditation in which anxiety, and its attendant autonomic arousal, diminish. This in turn reduces pain, lowers blood pressure, relieves depression, and promotes healing. However, since these patients are not taught that guidance is available to them in that state, they aren't likely to ask for it, and they may even tune their guide out if she or he attempts to communicate.

Thus, people using this technique receive some of the benefits of meditation but not others. Whatever meditative practice you choose, remember that there is a source of divine wisdom and power within you that is eager to communicate, but it will seldom speak unless you invite it to do so.

How do you "invite" your guide to speak? Simply by being curious to find out what she or he has to say. Certainly it is a good idea to mentally ask for help and advice when you begin to meditate, but even if you don't formally do this, your guide is aware of your intentions and can tell when you are receptive.

Inner Guidance Meditation

If you do not presently use a meditation technique, you might want to try the following. Simply sit comfortably with your eyes closed and take a few deep, slow breaths. Then focus upon being right where you are, centering yourself in the present moment. Be aware of the rise and fall of your chest as you breathe, the way your body feels sitting in your chair, and the sounds and smells around you. As psychologist Fritz Perls put it, "Lose your mind and come to your senses."

As thoughts arise in your consciousness, simply notice them — "Oh, a thought about dinner" — and then peacefully return to the experience of "being here, now." Try not to go off on a train of thought as you ordinarily would. And if you find you have, just release it and return to the here and now.

At first, you'll find that you go off on many tangents, realizing only much later that you've done so. Learning to consciously control one's attention is a challenging process, and you should not expect instant success. With practice, you will learn to go into a very peaceful and detached meditative state the moment you decide to do so. Just don't make the mistake of getting mad at yourself for becoming distracted. Since anger is a function of the ego, you'd have to leave meditation and reidentify with your ego to do that.

In any case, there is no need to wait for complete success in this first stage of meditation before proceeding to the second. Your inner teacher is eager to communicate, and your inexperience can't interfere with the process unless you unconsciously want it to. All you really need is a little curiosity to hear what your guide has to say.

After focusing on your present experience for five minutes or so, invite your guide to appear to your inner vision and to sit in an imaginary chair across from you. Begin by leaving the chair empty and wait patiently to see who appears in response to your call. Don't become flustered if it isn't who or what you expected — simply play along with whatever comes. There will be plenty of time to conclude it was all nonsense afterward, if that is the case.

Don't Be Afraid to Use Your Imagination

Imagination is very closely related to psychic and spiritual awareness, so don't defeat yourself at the outset by trying to rigorously exclude it. A common reaction people have to getting in touch with guidance is, "But I'm just making this stuff up!" Be prepared in advance for the likelihood that it is going to seem like you are making up your conversation with your guide — at least until she or he says something you don't expect, agree with, or even understand.

If you wait patiently for five minutes or so and still no one appears to have joined you, assume that some anxiety or resistance on your part is interfering, and address your guide as if he or she had appeared. Explain the nature of your inquiry and ask for advice, leaving your question open-ended so that there is wide latitude for response. For example, "What can I do about my financial problems?" is a better question than "How can I get my boss to give me a raise?" because it permits your inner teacher to put things into a larger perspective. Maybe there is no way to get your boss to give you a raise, and the thing you need to do is to find a different job. Maybe your financial difficulties are the result of attitudes toward money that must be changed before any improvement will be possible. Be open to anything that comes to you, remembering that you will evaluate it later.

I'd also advise you to avoid questions that can be answered with a yes or a no, since this makes it all too easy for your ego to masquerade as your inner teacher. If you require your guide to lay out his or her reasoning, you can make your own decision about whether the response is intelligent, loving, and otherwise consistent with a genuinely spiritual worldview.

Sometimes people will find themselves blocked, and report that their guide is not replying to their questions. If this happens to you, just say to yourself, "If my guide *could have* gotten through to me, what would my guide have said?" Make up whatever occurs to you as your guide's most likely reply, bearing in mind that it must reflect an unconditionally loving attitude toward everyone. Then continue the dialogue by responding as if what you imagined had really been said.

This ploy of asking yourself what *would have* happened if you were not blocking the response can be surprisingly effective. The truth is that if you are asking your guide for advice, he or she *has* replied, and you *are* receiving the answer at some level. You just aren't letting it into full consciousness.

Forced to make your best guess about what your guide would reply, you will very likely fall back on what you are dimly aware of, but don't really trust. It's important to realize that this process of perceiving guidance is extremely subtle. That's why your mind must be so still to do it. If you are waiting for the booming voice of Charlton Heston as Moses, and your guide responds instead with a whimsical remark, you're likely to discount what you've heard. Take seriously whatever comes to you — write it down — and perhaps on closer examination it will turn out to be more meaningful than you initially thought.

Remember, too, that your guide may not communicate

as a voice, especially if you wouldn't be comfortable with the idea of a voice speaking to you in your mind. Telepathy is a much more natural form of communication than words, and inspiration often comes in the form of images or ideas. Thoughts simply occur to us, and it is up to us to clothe them in words. I think you'll discover that if you put the wrong words to an idea your inner teacher is trying to communicate, it will be immediately apparent that it doesn't feel quite right, and you'll find yourself groping for a more accurate way of expressing it.

Use Your Own Best Judgment before Acting

Especially in the beginning, you should expect to have trouble telling whether or not a given message is truly coming from your divine companion spirit. Don't ignore common sense or risk your health or savings on something that might or might not be legitimate guidance. You have a responsibility to use your best judgment in this as in all things. Your inner teacher will not lead you wrong, but your ego loves to masquerade as God, and it will lead you wrong every time.

We have only to look at mental illness and religious fanaticism to realize that people can quite easily delude themselves about what God is directing them to do. There continue to be folks who commit terrorist acts in God's name, as well as ones who appear to sincerely believe that God is asking them to shun, despise, and persecute individuals of other religions, races, and sexual orientations. Only practice, coupled with your own good judgment, will allow you to reliably distinguish the voice of your inner teacher from the many voices of your ego.

On the other hand, if you let your ego be the final judge of every inner prompting, you'll surely defeat your own purpose. This is because our egos are often so confused about what the problem really is that they have trouble even recognizing an inspired solution, much less generating one. Take the following example.

SUSAN: WORDS SHE NEEDED TO HEAR

Once, early in my work as a psychotherapist, a woman I'll call Susan came to see me. Several years before, her daughter had nearly died from a severe electrical shock. The two-year-old stopped breathing, and a neighbor had wanted to begin artificial respiration immediately. Susan, in her panic, was afraid that his amateur attempts at first aid would only make things worse. She insisted upon waiting for the paramedics to arrive. When they did, they were able to resuscitate the child, but by then she had suffered severe brain damage as a result of prolonged oxygen deprivation. Susan's daughter had been in a persistent vegetative state ever since, unable to recognize anyone, communicate, or perform the simplest functions for herself.

I was then an intern, just learning to do psychotherapy. I knew that this loving mother must have been in torment over her disastrous decision to put off artificial respiration, and I was determined to tread very lightly in this area until a good therapeutic relationship had been established. It seemed crucial that I say nothing that would suggest that I thought she'd made a terrible mistake. So I was quite annoyed during one session when a sentence kept forming in my mind that pointed out what an awful blunder Susan had made, and how guilty she must feel about it.

The sentence actually made no literal sense that I could see. It didn't even seem grammatically correct. But it touched upon Susan's responsibility in the matter of her daughter's disability in what seemed to me to be a very blunt and offensive manner. Although this statement continued to resonate in my mind, I took a certain pride in my refusal to articulate it. "I might not be a very experienced therapist," I remember thinking, "but thank God I know better than to say something like that!"

Unfortunately, from that point on, the session began to go downhill. Not that anything in particular happened. It just dried up. My previous few sessions with Susan had been characterized by a lively exchange of ideas, but suddenly neither of us had anything to say to one another. In psychotherapy, there are good silences and bad silences, but the one Susan and I eventually fell into was the worst I've ever experienced.

As the awkwardness dragged on, I groped in vain for some new starting place. I had a growing conviction that at the end of the session Susan would make some polite excuse not to come back, and I was dismayed to realize that I would be relieved if she did. Anything was better than the barren sense of futility that had suddenly breached our developing relationship.

And through it all, that annoying sentence kept echoing in my head. How was I going to think of anything to say with that infernal racket going on? Finally, desperate to break the silence and no longer caring how I did it, I blurted out the words that had been demanding my attention. Strangely enough, I can no longer remember what they were. To me, the sentence was just a semimeaningless string of words.

To my surprise, Susan did not appear to be offended by my comment. Instead, she took on a thoughtful expression and started off on a new verbal tack. The session picked up energy, and she really began to open up. We finished on a very upbeat note, and our subsequent therapeutic work was exciting and productive.

Several weeks later, Susan said shyly, "Carolyn, do you remember that session a while back when we had that long silence?"

I said that I certainly did, and we both laughed about how awkward it had been. Then Susan went on: "And remember when you said...?" She repeated that peculiar sentence word for word. I was frankly surprised that she could so accurately remember an ungrammatical string of words.

"Uh oh!" I thought. "Here it comes. She really was offended and she's just getting around to telling me how insensitive I was. Well, I guess I have it coming."

But then Susan continued, "You know, when you said that, that's when I knew that you really understood, and that I could tell you everything. I had been all set to just quit therapy because I realized that I could never bring myself to tell someone else the truth about how I really felt about my daughter's accident. It just seemed hopeless. And then you said what you did, and I saw that it was all right to talk about it with you, because you already knew and yet you didn't hate me. I've been thinking about it for weeks, and I just had to tell you how much it meant to me that you said that."

This was a case where my guide handed me the key that would unlock a client's innermost thoughts, but my ego was not in a position to understand its value and would have cast it aside unused. As you learn to listen to your inner guide, be attentive to the possibility that impressions coming to you might mean more than they initially seem to. Proceed with care, but don't let your ego dismiss potentially valuable insights out of hand on the grounds that they are obviously mistaken.

To give one more example, consider the case of Anna.

Anna: "You Can't Do Anything Right!"

My client Anna and I were discussing her feelings of inadequacy. I reminded her of some very significant accomplishments in her life, and although she could acknowledge them, whatever self-esteem they inspired never went very deep or lasted very long. She had an abiding sense of incompetence and little hope about ever succeeding at anything.

At that point it occurred to me that her mother had drummed this idea into her head during childhood. A picture formed in my mind of Anna's mother sneering at her childish clumsiness and contemptuously saying: "You can't do anything right!" I assumed that it might be guidance and proposed the scenario to my client.

"Anna, I'm getting the feeling that perhaps your mother made you feel inadequate, starting from when you were very young. I seem to hear her saying, "You can't do anything right!" over and over again whenever you spilled milk, or tripped, or got your clothes dirty, or didn't move fast enough to suit her. Am I on track here?"

My client paused and looked thoughtful, but then she shook her head.

"I don't think so, Carolyn. I don't ever remember her saying that."

Well, that was good enough for me. If the image in my mind had been correct and really was at the root of Anna's problems, I would have expected her to remember these shaming events vividly and to react to them with a good deal of emotion. I was ready to move on.

My guide, however, was not. As I searched my mind for further inspiration, all I got was a more insistent version of the idea of Anna's mother saying, "You can't do anything right!" I reminded my guide that Anna was the best judge of whether this was true, and she had said it wasn't. This didn't seem like the sort of thing anyone would repress, and I had no doubt that Anna had thought about my question carefully and answered it honestly. There was no reason to stay with this line of inquiry. But I couldn't get rid of the idea that it was true, and that it was vital that Anna recognize that she'd been conditioned to think of herself as a failure for reasons that had nothing to do with her real abilities. Taking another stab at it, I waffled a bit.

"Is it possible that it wasn't your mother who said this, but some other powerful woman from childhood, like an aunt or a grandmother? Did anyone else constantly tell you that you couldn't do anything right?"

Anna thought about it for thirty seconds or so and then shrugged. "I don't ever remember anyone saying that to me, Carolyn." She looked a little sorry to disappoint me, but clearly she regarded my inquiry as misguided.

Considering the matter settled, I was once again ready to move on, but still the images in my mind insisted it had happened, and that it would be a mistake to give up on it. I felt completely frustrated. "Asked and answered!" I reprimanded my guide like a courtroom judge taking a lawyer to task. "She says it never happened, and she ought to know. Let's move on."

But the thoughts and images wouldn't go away. I sighed deeply and struggled to see if there was any way to reconcile my guidance with Anna's total inability to remember any such thing. Then I recalled that she had been raised in a Spanish-speaking home. In the spirit of a last resort, I tried one more time. Groping for fragments of Spanish I'd learned decades earlier, I said: "Anna, did your mother ever say anything like, '¡No puedes hacer nada!'"

It was as if an electric shock went through her. Her body straightened and her eyes became large and round.

"Jesus Christ, Carolyn!" she exploded. "If my mother said that to me once, she said it eight million times! All through my childhood, that's all me and my sisters ever heard! '¡No puedes hacer nada! ¡No puedes hacer nada!'" She mimicked her mother in a high-pitched, annoying whine, her face assuming the contemptuous sneer I'd been seeing on her mother's face in my mind's eye.

"That fucking bitch! She never once said anything to make us feel good about ourselves. No matter what we did, it was always, '¡No puedes hacer nada!' My sisters and I joke about it sometimes. One of us will screw up, and the others will all chorus, '¡No puedes hacer nada!' and we'll laugh our asses off. We can laugh about it now, but God how it hurt every time she said that!" Anna dissolved in tears and began to rage against her mother. It was a long time before she could calm down. When she did, her first concern was to apologize for being so obtuse earlier.

"Jesus, Carolyn, I'm sorry. When you said it in English, it just didn't compute. But you're right! No wonder I feel the way I do, when my mother told me I was a complete fuck-up every day of my life. It had nothing to do with me, personally. My mother was mean to everybody, whether they deserved it or not. She was just a bitch who never had a kind word for anyone."

Any Future Prediction Is Conditional

When you suspect that you *have* received divine guidance, remember that life is an improvisation involving many people. Your guide, like a good psychic, may be able to predict events in the short-term future with some considerable degree of accuracy. But the moment anyone involved experiences a real change of mind, the future being "unfolded" by that mind changes. For that reason, you should regard your guide's future predictions as "likely to come true, given that everyone involved continues on his or her present course." You need to stay in touch with events, seek further guidance as the situation develops, and remain poised to change course if necessary. Don't bet the farm that any prediction or recommendation your guide makes will turn out exactly as stated — although, of course, it might.

Things to Think About

1) The voice of your guide will be calm, respectful, and wise — never alarming, demeaning, blaming, or validating of your anger toward others.

2) If you can't hear your guide, it's because you don't yet really want to. Look for the fears that may be leading you to block communication.

3) If you have trouble making contact with your guide, feel free to begin by "making up" what you think your guide might say. This frees you from self-censorship and allows your thoughts to flow more freely.

4) Don't be too quick to conclude that the guidance you've received is defective. Later, it may mean more than it seems to now.

Chapter Fifteen

What Is a Miracle?

Every response you make to everything you perceive
is up to you, because your will determines
your perception of it.

— *Rajpur*

*N*ow I'd like to focus more closely on the shift in perception that constitutes a miracle and that *sometimes* produces results in the physical world that people call *miraculous*.
Remember, the actual miracle is not the healed body or
the peaceful outcome to a dangerous situation. It is *the unconditionally loving state of mind that allows such things to happen* when they are otherwise possible but highly unlikely.
Even when there is no observable effect of the miracle in the
physical world, *miracle-mindedness* is still of inestimable
value to the individual because he or she will be at peace no
matter what occurs.

DAVID: REPEATEDLY DISAPPOINTED

A man I'll call David moved with his family to Hawaii, a place they all loved. David got into a business deal there with a man I'll call Evan and eventually wound up in a legal conflict with his partner. Evan interpreted their contract in a way that would cost David dearly, and although David repeatedly approached his partner in a friendly way to seek some equitable resolution to their problem, Evan steadfastly refused to cooperate.

David explored his legal options but learned that bringing suit to recover the money he would lose would cost almost as much as he'd recover, and it would take too much time away from his family and other professional pursuits. He ultimately decided not to fight for his rights, gave up the idea of making a living in Hawaii, and moved his family back to the mainland United States, where they started over. He let go of his resentment about the situation and put his energy into building a new business.

And that's the end of the story.

Does this story sound like David was in touch with guidance while these events were occurring, including his move to Hawaii? Do you see evidence of any miracle here? If so, where?

I know David, and I believe he was in touch with his inner teacher throughout. Yet the guidance he received did not prevent him from becoming involved in the business deal; it did not find a way for him to work things out with his partner; nor did it find a way for his family to stay in Hawaii, where they would have preferred to remain.

Now you're probably thinking, "Is that really the best David's divine guide could do for him?" The answer, I suspect, is yes. First, we know that because we all have free will, people's behavior is not totally predictable. There may have been no way for David's guide to foresee the problems that were to arise with Evan. Once conflict did surface, the free will of everyone involved may have meant that there was no move David could have made to induce Evan to change his mind. Similarly, while David could have fought for his rights in court, any legal recourse he might have had would have involved an unacceptable expenditure of time, money, and stress, with no guarantee of success. So, back to the mainland he went.

Perhaps this seems like a disappointing conclusion. So far, I've been focusing upon fairly spectacular success stories involving miracles and guidance. In so doing, I may have given the impression that if you achieve miracle-mindedness and consult with your guide, you can get any situation to work out the way you want it to. This is not the case.

First of all, God and we Children of God constitute a family. A loving parent does not constantly favor one child — even a very good and obedient one — at the expense of others. The world exists to provide everyone opportunities for desired experiences, and that means that you aren't going to win everything you try for or avoid all injustice.

Not only may your ego's goals conflict with those of others, and be incompatible with the current state of the larger, consensual illusion — they may conflict with Reality as God is Being It. Remember what I said earlier about possible futures. You always have a number of them, but by no means everything you might wish to experience is immediately possible, given your present circumstances. This means that *there are going to be times when there is no way to achieve your goals*. All you can do at such times is cut your losses and move on, as David did.

Your inner guide can help you recognize your best move, given the limitations imposed by others and by conditions in the world, but he or she isn't going to be able to help you get what you want every time — unless what you want is inner peace, and its eternal companions, love and joy. Fortunately, that's what David did want, and by following his guide's advice to accept the financial setback, forgive Evan, and move to a place where his remaining money would go a little further, he made the best of a bad situation. The events were what they were, but it was up to David whether to seethe with shame and resentment, waste time on costly and possibly futile efforts to correct the situation, or shrug it off lightly and get on with his life.

So there *was* a miracle in David's story, and it lay in his decision to forgive and remain at peace despite the setback. Miracles make life heavenly, not by magically compelling everyone and everything to behave as we think they should, but by allowing us to be *just fine* whatever happens. This lesson was brought home to me in a very powerful way when my dog Wooley Bear became so old and sick that I reluctantly decided to take him to the veterinarian to be euthanized.

ME AND WOOLEY BEAR

Now if ever a person loved a dog, I loved Wooley. He had been my constant companion for fourteen years. Together we'd hitchhiked around the country, repeatedly moving from one place to another. Without Wooley, loneliness would have been an even bigger problem than it was. He'd loved me, protected me, and constantly amused and delighted me. I'd often wondered how I could ever face losing him, so my expectation at his death was that I would be in for a long period of intense mourning.

The day I took him to be put down, he was so weak and crippled with arthritis that he wasn't able to get to his feet in the vet's waiting room. With the vet's help I carried him inside, placed him on the examination table, and held him in my arms as he received the lethal injection. And then it was over and Wooley was gone.

Knowing how upset I'd be, I'd timed the veterinary appointment in such a way that it would allow me to just make it to a meditation group I attended regularly. I cried all the way there in the car.

However, as soon as the meditation began, in my mind's eye I saw Wooley racing through mountain meadows in pursuit of rabbits. He looked young and vigorous and completely happy doing what dogs love to do. He simply radiated a sense of wonder and relief at being freed from that crippled, blind, aching old body.

I experienced a deep certainty that Wooley was delighted with the change and that he felt nothing but love for me. All guilt about having had my best friend "put to sleep" vanished, and I discovered that I felt joyous and liberated, too.

To my further surprise, I never had another moment's sorrow about his passing. Having once looked at the matter from the perspective of my right mind, I realized that it was timely and appropriate that we both move on in different directions. After all those years, one of the things I'd dreaded most had finally happened to me, *and it wasn't the least bit distressing*.

I believe that my ability to accept the loss of my dog with no sense of pain or regret was a miracle. Had I allowed my consciousness to remain at the level of my ego, I know I would have suffered horribly over Wooley's death, as so many people do when they lose a beloved animal companion. Once I shifted into miracle-mindedness, it was possible for my guide to show me that there was really nothing to be sad about.

SUFFERING IS OPTIONAL

Miracles relieve suffering, even when they don't change the circumstances that seem to be the cause of suffering. The truth is that circumstances are never the problem, in and of themselves. It is always and only our ego's misperceptions about what's happening that make it pleasant or painful. And perception always involves choice.

Good and *bad* are simply labels our egos paste onto an event that just "is." Indeed, as lecturer and spiritual teacher Patricia Sun[1] points out, the words *wonderful* and *awful* actually mean much the same thing. Full of wonder. Full of awe. Both describe an experience that is powerful and mysterious that we can't understand, but we use *awful* when we've decided it is appropriate to be afraid of it, and *wonderful* when we greet it with positive expectation. Consider, for example, the following parable from ancient China.

The Wanderer Returns

A traveler returns to his native village and is warmly greeted by his neighbor. Eager to catch up on local affairs, the returning man asks the other what's been going on since he left.

"Well," the neighbor replies. "You remember that horse I had? A couple of months ago he broke down the pasture fence and ran away."

"That's awful!" the traveler responds with immediate sympathy.

"Not really," the other man responds. "You see, he came back a few days later and he brought a whole herd of wild mares with him. Now I have ten horses!"

"That's wonderful!" exclaims the traveler.

"Not so wonderful," the neighbor replies. "You see, my son was trying to ride one of the mares. She threw him and he broke his leg."

"That's awful!" says the returned traveler.

"Not so awful," his friend goes on. "You see, the following week the army came through here and conscripted all of the young men of the village to fight in the Emperor's wars. But they couldn't take my son because he had a broken leg."

At the level of our egos we have no idea what the ultimate consequences of any event will turn out to be. A situation such as a divorce that seems tragic at the time may later look like the best thing that ever happened to us. Nevertheless, egos feel entitled to judge everything based upon their own limited points of view, and to be miserable when things they've chosen to view as *bad* occur. If we're identifying with our egos, we'll suffer right along with them.

This is what the Buddha meant when he said that the

roots of suffering are *clinging* and *aversion*. At the level of our egos, we imagine that our happiness depends upon having things the way we think they *should* be. We cling to some experiences — like having Wooley Bear around, or living in Hawaii — and imagine we'd have to feel devastated if they ever changed. We wear ourselves out trying to avoid experiences our egos have labeled *awful*, as if losing a job or being embarrassed in public would be the end of the world.

When we are miracle-minded, everything slips back into true perspective, and we realize that illusions can never really hurt us. We stop taking everything so personally, and the whole rich tapestry of life becomes acceptable — even the parts that involve some personal inconvenience in the service of a larger good. We realize that, at the level of our right minds, we fully endorse the movement of God, even though our ego doesn't like seeing what it regards as its "own" eggs broken to make God's latest omelet.

The miracle, then, is the perceptual shift that occurs when we decide to accept on faith a circumstance that is completely unacceptable to our ego. Instead of panicking or psychologically distancing themselves, miracle-minded individuals quiet their minds and tune in more closely. Like skillful surfers riding the ever-changing waves of creation, they "go with the flow." Their poise in the face of what the ego deems a calamity is the miracle, whether or not it is followed by a beneficial change in the physical illusion.

CYNTHIA: DAMPENING ARDOR WITH HUMOR

Cynthia was returning to her Venice Beach apartment after attending a party in Los Angeles that had lasted into the early hours of the morning. She parked her car and was crossing the deserted lot when two men emerged from the shadows and seized her roughly.

"Hi, honey!" said one suggestively. "You're just in time to provide us with a little entertainment. Get those panties off, and let's go!" One man grabbed at her breast while the other maneuvered around behind her. Both made vulgar and thoroughly graphic comments about her body and the things they were planning to do to her.

The beach where Cynthia's apartment was located was always teeming with homeless men who made the area very dangerous at night. These two were shabbily dressed and had obviously been drinking. Cynthia knew that she wasn't going to be able to outrun them over gravel in her spike heels even if she could get free. And, although there were undoubtedly people sleeping in nearby apartments, the embattled residents would know better than to get involved in her problems if she screamed. Violence was a common nighttime occurrence in Venice, and Cynthia was about to become its next victim.

"I became very calm," Cynthia told me. "I could see that I was going to be raped — there was nothing I could realistically hope to do about that. It just seemed like there was no point in getting upset about something that was inevitable.

"And when I accepted that, my mind moved on to the next thing — which was that as bad as it was going to be to be raped by these two creeps, it was even worse to think of it happening here on the gravel in the parking lot. Not only would I be raped, I would also wind up scraped and filthy, and my beautiful new dress would be ruined!

"So I said, 'Hey! If you're going to rape me, get it over with! But let's not do it here. My apartment is right over there. You can at least have the decency to rape me somewhere clean and comfortable!'

"That really threw those guys for a loop. They both burst out laughing, and one of them said, 'Boy! You've really got balls, lady!'

"'Hey, this is a new dress and it cost *beaucoup* bucks!' I returned. 'Anything happens to this dress, and you guys'll wish you'd never been born! Got that?'

"'Got it, lady. We sure wouldn't want to get *you* mad at us. No sirree. You're one tough mama. Lead the way.'"

As they walked to her apartment, Cynthia began to banter with the men. They were obviously tickled by her self-assertiveness. The idea of a rape victim calling the shots was clearly a new experience for them. Cynthia has a wonderful, biting wit, and as she exchanged humorous barbs with her assailants, ideas of rape seemed to recede into the background. By the time they reached her door, the atmosphere was downright friendly.

"It was like they were buddies of mine walking me home," Cynthia recalls. "One of them was still laughing about me being such a ballsy chick, and the other was giving me a brotherly warning to be more careful next time. A pretty woman like me ought not to be out alone after dark in this neighborhood. Didn't I know there were a lot of dangerous characters hanging around? All I can tell you is that it was really bizarre!"

When they reached her apartment, Cynthia unlocked her door. "So, are you guys coming in?" she asked.

"Naw," one replied. "I guess we'll just be getting along. You have a good night now. And be a little more careful next time. Not everybody out here is as nice as us."

The Serenity Prayer says: God grant me the serenity to accept the things I cannot change, the courage to change the things I can, and the wisdom to know the difference.

Cynthia realized that the only thing she could do about her situation was to refuse to go into fear and suffer over it. Opting for serenity (miracle-mindedness), she found a way to peacefully accept the things she couldn't see any way to change, as well as the courage to take a stab at changing the things she might be able to influence. In the process, she offered these men an opportunity to play the role of friends rather than assailants, and they gladly took her up on it.

What I want to emphasize is that this choice in favor of inner peace would have been every bit as much a miracle even if Cynthia had been raped. Her decision not to suffer over her misfortune would have minimized the awfulness of it, and it would have speeded her physical and psychological recovery, even if nothing resembling divine intervention was visible to others. Even when miracle-mindedness does not alter the course of negative events in the physical realm, it lifts the Child of God above the battlefield where he or she feels comforted and protected.

Things to Think About

1) The miracle lies in your choice to maintain your serenity, no matter what.

2) Miracles may or may not influence the course of events in the physical world.

3) Whether or not they improve the objective situation, miracles always make you feel better.

4) Miracles cannot be used to get the world to conform to your ego's expectations.

Chapter Sixteen

Test-Driving Miracle-Mindedness

We spend a great deal of time telling God what
we think should be done and not enough time waiting in the
stillness for God to tell us what to do.

— Peace Pilgrim[1]

*I*n the final analysis, you have two choices. You can treat
miracles as just another interesting issue that has not yet
been fully resolved and file this book away on your bookshelf
under *M* (for miracles, Miller, or madness, as you prefer).
Or you can take matters into your own hands and find out
for yourself if divine grace is real by becoming miracle-
minded and referring some of your own problems to your
inner teacher for solution. This latter approach requires you
to become an investigator yourself, designing personal experiments that will establish the reality of miracles to your own
satisfaction.

All this really means is that you are going to try doing

something different, in order to see if things work out differently as a result. Begin with a situation where you feel threatened, whether physically, financially, emotionally, or whatever. When you are tempted to retaliate, or to regard yourself as a victim, try a miracle-minded approach instead.

The first step is to pause and recognize that you don't really know what your best move is, despite your ego's conviction that you should lash out, placate the aggressor, or display your pain and indignation in an attempt to induce guilt. Instead of following any of your ego's proposals, try silently turning within to seek divine guidance.

Quiet your mind and mentally reach for a new, more loving perspective on what is happening. You might even ask yourself the question, "What would Love do now?" And when some other way of handling the situation occurs to you, speak and act in accord with this perspective and see whether things turn out better than you initially thought they would. You can use your whole lifetime of prior experience with non-miracle-minded approaches to similar problems for purposes of comparison. Perhaps an example will make this clearer:

TIFFANY: MY SEVEREST CRITIC

My master's level class in personality theories was constantly being disrupted by a particularly contentious student. Tiffany was a bright woman in her late twenties, but she seemed convinced that I was trying to put something over on the students and that it was her duty to spearhead the opposition to this oppression.

No matter what the topic, I could always count on Tiffany to heatedly contradict whatever I had just said. Any time I pointed out the benefits of a certain approach, she "exposed" it for what it "really" was. She was loudly denouncing my "inexcusable ignorance" and "reactionary views" several times at each class meeting.

These continual verbal confrontations took a certain emotional toll on me. For one thing, it was a struggle to keep the discussion on track in the face of Tiffany's constant efforts to subvert it. And, naturally, it was not pleasant to be treated with hostility and contempt. At the level of my ego, I felt insulted by her attitude and regarded myself as her innocent victim. I realized that I could use my legitimate authority as the teacher to insist that Tiffany behave in a more appropriate manner "or else," but something held me back from pursuing this obvious solution.

Tiffany clearly believed that her withering comments reflected what everyone else was really thinking. I could see that she expected the other students to rally to her and that she interpreted their failure to do so as evidence of the degree to which they had been intimidated and brainwashed. However, I knew that many of her classmates were fed up with her behavior.

Other students would come up after class or drop in to my office to disassociate themselves from her sentiments. In fact, one grandmotherly woman facetiously threatened that the next time Tiffany took that tone with me, she was going to personally drag her out into the hall and slap some sense into her! Several offered to take Tiffany aside and try to persuade her to behave more appropriately, but we agreed that

that would only make her feel attacked and defensive. I suggested that they leave the matter to me.

Following my inner guidance, I adopted a very permissive policy, allowing Tiffany to express her uncomplimentary views in full. When she had finished her denunciation, I would say something nonjudgmental, such as, "Well, you've raised some interesting points, Tiffany, and I'm sure everyone will want to think about what you've said." Then I would go on with the business of the class. I tried to treat her with friendly courtesy, to avoid direct confrontation, and to convey that it was perfectly all right for her to disagree with me.

Unfortunately, this approach didn't seem to be getting me anywhere. The verbal attacks did not lessen in either frequency or intensity. I couldn't help feeling that I must be doing something wrong, so I once again took the matter up with my guide in meditation.

"What do you think I ought to do about Tiffany?" I asked. "She seems so angry with me. Am I doing something to cause this?"

"What you're doing is fine," Jesus responded. "This is her own problem with authority. Tiffany thinks of you as someone who has power, and she believes that the quickest way to get some for herself is to take yours. In her mind, if she can tear you down in front of the class, everyone will admire her and look to her for leadership. She unconsciously considers the students your followers, and she wants to win them for herself by defeating you in 'single combat.'

"If she could get you to fight back, then she could use your repressive response as the pretext for her own hostility. When you don't defend yourself or even acknowledge that you've been attacked, it confuses her and may eventually lead her to see what she is doing."

But this explanation didn't really satisfy me. I couldn't let go of the feeling that I must be doing something wrong.

"But, look," I said. "If I'm really doing it 100 percent right, why isn't it working? I must be doing something wrong. If I'm truly being totally nondefensive with Tiffany, why doesn't she notice that I'm not her enemy and stop attacking me? If my motives are innocent enough, shouldn't she get it that I'm not trying to hurt her, and stop trying to hurt me?"

"Well," Jesus shrugged, "they crucified *me*."

This bland statement hit me like a cold shower. Of course! How silly of me to think that the truth would always prevail in the short run! If a great spiritual master like Jesus couldn't make people understand something they didn't want to understand, what made me think that I was going to be able to instantly transform Tiffany's whole orientation toward authority? After all, she had free will, too. If she chose to construct a personal illusion in which she was victimized by authority figures, she was free to do so. All I could do was to continue confounding her expectation of counterattack. It was up to her what, if any, conclusion she drew from that.

This conversation relieved the lingering sense of inadequacy I'd been feeling over these outbursts. From then on, it was much clearer in my mind. I would pray for Tiffany's eventual enlightenment and do my part as well as I could. It was up to Tiffany if, and when, she would withdraw the insulting projections she was placing upon me.

The course ended with no sign of improvement in her

attitude. I was aware of having to exercise extra vigilance to prevent Tiffany's openly expressed contempt for me from influencing my academic evaluation of her performance in the class. I confess that it was a great relief to know that I had seen the last of this troublesome student.

One day between quarters as I was working in my office, Tiffany came in and tearfully asked if she could speak with me. She was deeply troubled about a personal problem, she said, and I was the only person she felt comfortable sharing it with. She needed some advice, and there was no one else on the faculty she could really trust — no one who understood her as I did. I was stunned to discover that she now regarded me as a respected friend and ally!

Further evidence of this inner transformation came shortly thereafter. When the next quarter began, Tiffany signed up for an elective course I was teaching, which she could quite easily have avoided altogether or taken from another professor. I am still amused to remember the expressions on the faces of the students who had been in the personality theories class the previous quarter. Many of them made no attempt to hide their astonishment when Tiffany walked in. Several nudged their neighbors to get their attention and then jerked their heads in Tiffany's direction, secretly exchanging comical glances of open-mouthed incredulity with me and one another.

Those of us who had witnessed her previous performance could scarcely believe the delightful change in Tiffany. From then on, she was invariably friendly and supportive toward me. Further, I soon realized that the inner transformations hadn't stopped with her. Several students commented privately that they felt they had learned a very profound lesson about the power of defenselessness through watching me handle my conflict with Tiffany. Some said that they had already put the new technique into practice and seen it transform a difficult relationship in their own lives. I realized belatedly that this confrontation had been a valuable learning experience for everyone present. What my ego had regarded as an unwarranted imposition turned out to be a priceless opportunity to learn the value of miracle-mindedness by teaching it to others.

Notice the way my miracle-minded attitude toward Tiffany ensured my own comfort and inner peace as she continued her hostile behavior. Once I got my ego out of the way, I went from outrage and indignation to feeling like I was dealing with a minor nuisance. From my point of view, this inner shift would have been worthwhile whether or not Tiffany ever relented toward me. Her eventual change in behavior — the only thing other people were able to observe — was a bonus. The actual miracle was something only I was in a position to know about, because I was the only one who could verify the relationship between what I was thinking, my personal comfort, and the things that happened around me.

Because the evidence for miracles rests on personal experience, the only way science can ever document them is through self-report. And, although self-report data are considered quite good enough to use in medical research and the social sciences, they aren't going to satisfy anyone convinced that people who believe in miracles are self-deluded. However, the fact that some folks will never believe you've created miracles needn't keep you from verifying their reality through informal personal experiments like my handling of Tiffany.

BELIEVE IN RESULTS, NOT THEORIES

As we've seen, science demands more than the sorts of anecdotal evidence of miracles we've looked at in this book to consider them substantiated. Nevertheless, this is how scientific research begins, and our questioning reflects precisely how the scientific mind works, informally testing intuitions about what's going on before investing time and money in closely controlled laboratory studies. Rigorous experimentation is actually one of the last steps in a long process of scientific thinking — a step that is necessary to persuade others of what the scientist believes she or he already knows on the basis of personal experience, intuition, and anecdotal evidence.

For example, in the United States in the early 1840s, Dr. Oliver Wendell Holmes was deeply concerned about the number of women who died of puerperal fever while giving birth. He noticed that this happened much more often when the attending physician had come directly from performing autopsies in the morgue without washing his hands in between. Although the concept of infection was poorly understood, it occurred to Holmes that there might be some invisible "contagion" the doctors picked up on their hands from corpses and then transferred to the women during delivery. Up to this point, his approach was purely observational and intuitive.

Holmes informally tested his theory by persuading the doctors at the hospital where he was working to wash their hands after performing autopsies, and he was rewarded by a dramatic drop in the incidence of puerperal fever. This provided anecdotal evidence of the efficacy of hand washing in preventing this deadly scourge.

Had he been working today, Holmes would probably have gone on to perform an actual experiment, randomly assigning doctors to Washing and No-Washing groups, controlling or randomizing potentially confounding variables such as the physician's education and degree of professional experience, and analyzing the results for statistical significance.

There is no comparable experimental design to use in evaluating miracles, partly because hand washing is publicly observable, while we would have to take someone's word for the presence or absence of miracle-mindedness. Then, too, while a miraculous shift in perception is guaranteed to comfort and relieve the individual who makes it, there is no way to predict what — if any — change it will make in the situation itself. The physical means by which positive outcomes appear to be effected are often totally unexpected. One would-be assailant has a change of heart, while another is tossed aside by some unseen force, and another is soundly thrashed by a frail young woman. Who would have hypothesized there would be a brand-new beaver pond right where it was needed, or that an inner voice would emerge to direct one out of harm's way? Truly, God does move in mysterious ways! The only prediction possible in an experiment on miracles would be that things would turn out much better for someone who reports miracle-mindedness than he or she could have imagined possible, and that is fairly vague and subjective for the tastes of most scientists.

But that doesn't mean you can't go as far as Holmes went. Just remember that in the case of miracles, the independent variable — *the thing you are doing differently* — is the shift into a peaceful, unconditionally loving state of consciousness. And the dependent variable — *the thing you expect to see happen* — is that you'll achieve a sense of inner peace with situations that might have been eating you up with anxiety or resentment or futile attempts to compel others to change. Remember that where miracles are concerned, the "proof of the pudding" is indeed "in the tasting" — not in the judgments of observers.

Of course, outside observers usually do notice a very positive change in someone who opts for miracle-mindedness. Nevertheless, your state of consciousness may or may not produce visible results in the circumstances that prompted you to adopt it. Only you will know for sure if you performed a miracle. And in cases where there is no visible result, only you will know how much you gained from doing so.

Oh! Perhaps I should add that hand washing didn't catch on. Holmes's colleagues regarded him as a crank for thinking that some sort of invisible agent caused disease. The same fate befell Dr. Ignaz Semmelweis a few years later in Europe, when he independently advanced a similar theory of contagion. Then, as now, some folks have trouble with the idea that things that can't be seen with the naked eye might nonetheless exert powerful effects within our world.

TEST-DRIVING MIRACLE-MINDEDNESS

No one would fault you if you test-drove a car before agreeing to purchase it. You would simply be a "wise consumer." All I'm suggesting is that you try out miracle-mindedness in the same way you might test an automobile. Simply follow the instructions for use in a conscientious manner and see whether it performs as advertised.

It's not necessary to wait for a life-or-death emergency. We all have problems and interpersonal conflicts. Start with small things, and as you get positive results, you'll have more confidence in approaching bigger ones. Remember that happy endings to dangerous and distressing situations exist only as potential until you make them real for yourself by "resting in peace," following inner guidance, and believing in the possibility of an outcome that benefits everyone.

And, finally, don't handicap yourself with the idea that you are not yet "spiritual" enough to hear the voice of your guide and create miracles. You are as much a Child of God as anyone else on the planet, you have a divine guide, and that guide is eager to make conscious contact with you. Each shift into miracle-mindedness benefits you psychologically and spiritually, whether or not it produces a physical result. The only way you can actually fail is by not making the attempt. Every moment devoted to miracle-mindedness succeeds beyond your wildest imaginings, so don't allow your ego to persuade you it isn't worth the effort.

Miracles not worth the effort? Come on now!

Notes

CHAPTER 1

1. Rick Warren, *The Purpose-Driven Life: What on Earth Am I Here For?* (Grand Rapids, MI: Zondervan, 2002).
2. Ashley Smith with Stacy Mattingly, *Unlikely Angel: The Untold Story of the Atlanta Hostage Hero* (Grand Rapids, MI: Zondervan, 2005).
3. "Ashley Smith's 'Unlikely Angel' " (interview with Ashley Smith by coanchor Rene Sylev), *The Early Show*, CBS News, October 5, 2005, http://www.cbsnews.com/stories/2005/10/04/earlyshow.
4. "Ga. Hostage Gave Drugs to Captor," CBS News/Associated Press, September 27, 2005, http://www.cbsnews.com/stories/2005/09/27/national/main887323_page2.shtml.
5. Ibid.

6. "Ex-Hostage Collects $70K Reward," CBS News/Associated Press, March 24, 2005, http://www.cbsnews.com/stories/2005/04/15/national/main688574.shtml.

7. C. S. Lewis, *Miracles: How God Intervenes in Nature and Human Affairs* (New York: Macmillan, 1947), 5.

8. "Official Report of the Lourdes Medical Commission," in Brendan O'Regan, "Healing, Remission, and Miracle Cures," in *Noetic Sciences Collection 1980–1990: Ten Years of Consciousness Research*, ed. Barbara McNeill and Carol Guion (Sausalito, CA: Institute of Noetic Sciences, 1991). For updates on the commission's work, visit lourdes-france.com.

Chapter 2

1. *A Course in Miracles* (Tiburon, CA: Foundation for Inner Peace, 1975).

2. My husband, Arnie Weiss, and I met through our mutual interest in the *Course*, and we subsequently created the nonprofit Foundation and Institute for the Study of *A Course in Miracles* in West Los Angeles. Through the foundation we offer study groups and psychotherapy (as described in the pamphlet on psychotherapy that was also channeled by Schucman and Thetford). To find out more, you might read my book *Soulmates: Following Inner Guidance to the Relationship of Your Dreams* (Novato, CA: H J Kramer Inc/New World Library, 2000).

Chapter 3

1. B.F. Skinner, *Beyond Freedom and Dignity* (New York: Alfred A. Knopf, 1971).

2. Farr A. Curlin and others, "Religious Characteristics of U.S. Physicians: A National Survey," *Journal of General Internal Medicine* 20, no. 7 (July 2005): 629–34.

3. Larry B. Stammer, "Physicist Wins Spirituality Prize," *Los Angeles Times*, March 10, 2005.

4. Joe Nickell, *Looking for a Miracle: Weeping Icons, Relics, Stigmata, Visions & Healing Cures* (Buffalo, NY: Prometheus Books, 1998).

5. John F. Fischer, "A Summary Critique of Analyses of the 'Blood' on the Turin 'Shroud,'" in Joe Nickell, *Inquest on the Shroud of Turin* (Buffalo, NY: Prometheus Books, 1983), 157–60.

6. Nickell, "Unshrouding a Mystery," in *Looking for a Miracle*, 296.

7. Raymond Rogers, "Studies on the Radiocarbon Sample from the Shroud of Turin," *Journal Thermochimica Acta* 425, no. 1–2 (2005): 189–94.

8. James M. Wood and M. Theresa Nezworski, "Science as a History of Corrected Mistakes," *American Psychologist* 60, no. 6 (September 2005): 657.

9. James Randi, *Flim-Flam! Psychics, ESP, Unicorns and Other Delusions* (Buffalo, NY: Prometheus Books, 1987).

CHAPTER 5

1. Michael Polanyi, *Personal Knowledge: Toward a Post-Critical Philosophy* (Chicago: University of Chicago Press, 1958), 24.

2. Polanyi, *Personal Knowledge*, 33.

3. C. G. Jung, *Synchronicity* (Princeton: Bollingen Paperbacks, 1973).

4. B. Bryson, Jr., "What's a Coincidence?" *American Way* (May 1982): 60–65.

CHAPTER 6

1. Bernie Siegel, *Love, Medicine and Miracles: Lessons Learned about Self-Healing from a Surgeon's Experience with Exceptional Patients* (New York: Harper & Row, 1986).

2. Stephen Kierulff and Stanley Krippner, *Becoming Psychic: Spiritual Lessons for Focusing Your Hidden Abilities* (Franklin Lakes, NJ: The Career Press, 2004).

3. Marc Barasch, "A Psychology of the Miraculous," *Psychology Today* (March/April 1994): 54–80.

4. O'Regan, *Noetic Sciences Collection*.
5. Gerald Jampolsky, *Teach Only Love: The Seven Principles of Attitudinal Healing* (New York: Bantam, 1983).
6. Barasch, "A Psychology of the Miraculous."
7. O'Regan, *Noetic Sciences Collection*.
8. O'Regan, *Noetic Sciences Collection*.
9. O'Regan, *Noetic Sciences Collection*.
10. Shakti Gawain, *Creative Visualization* (Mill Valley, CA: New World Library, 1978).
11. For more on the medical commission's procedures, visit their official website at lourdes-france.com.
12. "Official Report of the Lourdes Medical Commission," in O'Regan, *Noetic Sciences Collection*.
13. D. J. West, *Eleven Lourdes Miracles* (London: Duckworth, 1957).
14. Barasch, "A Psychology of the Miraculous."
15. Barasch, "A Psychology of the Miraculous."

CHAPTER 7

1. Barbara Hoberman Levine, *Your Mind Hears Every Word You Say* (Lower Lake, CA: Aslan Publishing, 1991).
2. R. J. Byrd, "Positive Therapeutic Effects of Intercessory Prayer in a Coronary Care Unit Population," *Southern Medical Journal* 81 (1988): 826–29.
3. W. S. Harris, M. Gowda, J. W. Kolb, and others, "A Randomized, Controlled Trial of the Effects of Remote, Intercessory Prayer on Outcomes in Patients Admitted to the Coronary Care Unit," *Archives of Internal Medicine* 159 (October 1999): 2273–78.
4. Daniel J. Benor, *Healing Research*, 2 vols. (Medford, NJ: Wholistic Healing Publications, 2005).
5. John T. Chibnall, Joseph M. Jeral, and Michael A. Cerullo, "Experiments on Distant Intercessory Prayer: God, Science, and the Lesson of Massah," *Archives of Internal Medicine* 161 (November 2001): 2529–36.

6. Chibnall, "Experiments on Prayer."
7. R. G. Jahn and B. J. Dunne, *Margins of Reality: The Role of Consciousness in the Physical World* (New York: Harcourt, Brace, Jovanovich, 1987).
8. Dean Radin and Roger Nelson, "Evidence for Consciousness-Related Anomalies in Random Physical Systems," *Foundations of Physics* 19 (1989): 1499–1514.
9. W. G. Braud and M.T. Schlitz, "Consciousness Interactions with Remote Biological Systems: Anomalous Intentional Effects." *Journal of Scientific Exploration* 2 (1991): 1–46.
10. Larry Dossey, *Space, Time & Medicine* (Boston: Shambhala Publications, Inc., 1982).

CHAPTER 9

1. Rajpur is the name used by an awakened being who channels through Paul Tuttle of the Northwest Foundation for *A Course in Miracles*, in Kingston, Washington. The entity purports to be Jesus Christ, author of *A Course in Miracles*. To find out more about "Raj," consult the website www.nwffacim.org.
2. Quoted in Gerald A. LaRue, *The Supernatural, the Occult, and the Bible* (Buffalo, NY: Prometheus Books, 1990), 117–18.

CHAPTER 10

1. Fritjof Capra, *The Tao of Physics* (New York: Bantam Books, 1975).
2. Norman Friedman, *Bridging Science and Spirit* (St. Louis: Living Lake Books, 1994), 21.
3. James Jeans, in Paramahansa Yogananda, *Autobiography of a Yogi* (Los Angeles: Self-Realization Fellowship, 1983), 314.
4. David Bohm, "A Conversation with David Bohm," interview by Renee Weber in *ReVision* 4 (1981).
5. Friedman, *Bridging Science and Spirit*, 26.
6. Serge King, *Mastering Your Hidden Self: A Guide to the Huna Way* (Wheaton, IL: Theosophical Publishing House, 1985), 9.

CHAPTER 11

1. Neale Donald Walsch, *Conversations with God: An Uncommon Dialogue*, vol. 1 (New York: Putnam Publishing Group, 1996), 106.

CHAPTER 14

1. Herbert Benson, *The Mind-Body Effect* (New York: Simon & Schuster, 1979).

CHAPTER 15

1. To read more about Patricia Sun, who lectures widely, visit her website, http://www.patriciasun.com.

CHAPTER 16

1. Peace Pilgrim, *Peace Pilgrim: Her Life and Works in Her Own Words* (Santa Fe: Ocean Tree, 1991).

About the Author

Carolyn Miller holds a PhD in experimental psychology, which she taught at both the graduate and undergraduate levels for more than twenty years. She has conducted research and published articles and books on a variety of subjects, ranging from the neurophysiology of weight regulation to the psychology of humor; from love relationships to miracles. Dr. Miller is currently a clinical psychologist practicing in West Los Angeles, where she lives with her husband, Arnold Weiss, PhD. She also teaches classes on *A Course in Miracles*.